Before Sunrise

I0061696

This book offers a fresh analysis of *Before Sunrise* that reframes its romance within the contexts of transnational culture and cinema. The book highlights the symbolic value of the film's construction of transnational youth in the building of a trans-European culture.

Engaging with the film's critical history, this book focuses on its specific view of youth and young love. *Before Sunrise: Young Love on the Move* examines young love within the cultural context of the 1990s in the US and its links with Generation X and the slacker culture. Within a wider scope, it also looks at the history and theory of romantic comedy and its connections with independent cinema. In considering the film a transnational text, this analysis underlines the parallels between a narrative of young love at the end of the 20th century and the construction of a young, or rejuvenated, Europe.

Before Sunrise: Young Love on the Move provides an invaluable insight into this beloved film for students and researchers in film studies, transnational cinema and youth culture.

María del Mar Azcona teaches Film Studies and English at the University of Zaragoza. Her research is about comedy, mobilities, cosmopolitanism and star studies. She is the author of *The Multi-Protagonist Film* (2010) and co-author, with Celestino Deleyto, of *Alejandro González Iñárritu* (2010).

Celestino Deleyto is Professor of Film Studies and English at the University of Zaragoza. His research fields include comedy, transnational cinema, cosmopolitan and border theory and film and social space. He is the author of *The Secret Life of Romantic Comedy* (2009), *From Tinseltown to Bordertown: Los Angeles on Film* (2016) and co-author, with María del Mar Azcona, of *Alejandro González Iñárritu* (2010).

Cinema and Youth Cultures

Cinema and Youth Cultures engages with well-known youth films from American cinema as well as the cinemas of other countries. Using a variety of methodological and critical approaches the series volumes provide informed accounts of how young people have been represented in film, while also exploring the ways in which young people engage with films made for and about them. In doing this, the Cinema and Youth Cultures series contributes to important and long-standing debates about youth cultures, how these are mobilized and articulated in influential film texts and the impact that these texts have had on popular culture at large.

Series Editors: Siân Lincoln and Yannis Tzioumakis

Lady Bird
Self-Determination for a New Century
Rob Stone

Mustang
Translating Willful Youth
Elif Akçalı, Cüneyt Çakırlar, Özlem Güçlü

Mary Poppins
Radical Elevation in the 1960s
Leslie H. Abramson

The Outsiders
Adolescent Tenderness and Staying Gold
Ann M. Ciasullo

American Graffiti
George Lucas, the New Hollywood and the Baby Boom Generation
Peter Krämer

Before Sunrise
Young Love on the Move
María del Mar Azcona and Celestino Deleyto

For more information about this series, please visit: https://www.routledge
.com/Cinema-and-Youth-Cultures/book-series/CYC

Before Sunrise

Young Love on the Move

María del Mar Azcona and Celestino Deleyto

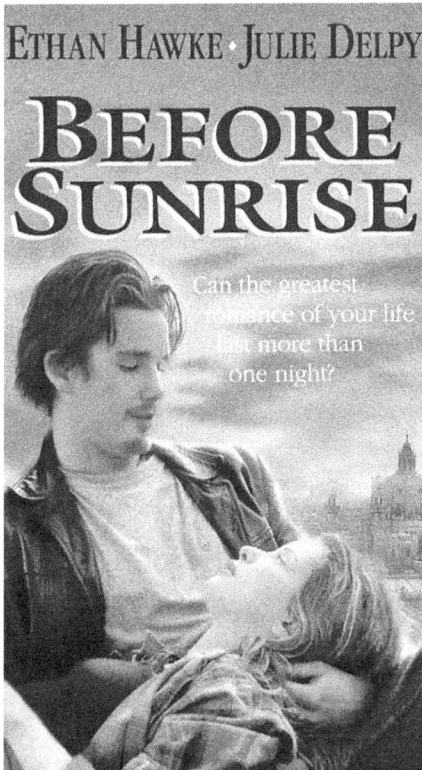

ETHAN HAWKE · JULIE DELPY

BEFORE SUNRISE

Can the greatest romance of your life last more than one night?

Routledge
Taylor & Francis Group

LONDON AND NEW YORK

First published 2023
by Routledge
4 Park Square, Milton Park, Abingdon, Oxon OX14 4RN

and by Routledge
605 Third Avenue, New York, NY 10158

Routledge is an imprint of the Taylor & Francis Group, an informa business

© 2023 María del Mar Azcona and Celestino Deleyto

The right of María del Mar Azcona and Celestino Deleyto
to be identified as authors of this work has been asserted
in accordance with sections 77 and 78 of the Copyright,
Designs and Patents Act 1988.

All rights reserved. No part of this book may be reprinted
or reproduced or utilised in any form or by any electronic,
mechanical, or other means, now known or hereafter
invented, including photocopying and recording, or in any
information storage or retrieval system, without permission
in writing from the publishers.

Trademark notice: Product or corporate names may be
trademarks or registered trademarks, and are used only for
identification and explanation without intent to infringe.

British Library Cataloguing-in-Publication Data
A catalogue record for this book is available from the British
Library

ISBN: 978-1-032-12392-9 (hbk)
ISBN: 978-1-032-12393-6 (pbk)
ISBN: 978-1-003-22433-4 (ebk)

DOI: 10.4324/9781003224334

Typeset in Times New Roman
by Deanta Global Publishing Services, Chennai, India

Contents

List of figures   *vii*
Series Editors' Introduction   *viii*
Acknowledgements   *x*

Introduction: Out of the Past   1

1   **Youth Cultures in the 1990s**   4

Strangers on a Train 4
'Talkin' 'bout My Generation' 5
Cut Them Some Slack 10

2   **Indie, Comic and Transnational: The Production of**
    ***Before Sunrise* in Context**   14

Linklater and the Journey of Indie Cinema in the 1990s 14
A Philadelphia Story 16
Erasing Romcom 17
Gender, Desire and Dialogue 20
Coming to Europe 22

3   **Falling in Love with Linklater: Genre, Realism,**
    Quotation and Young Love   25

Pink Champagne 25
'Later' 28
'Let's Just Be Rational Adults About This' 33

4   **Crossing the Ocean: From Regional to Transnational**   39

The Journey to the Border 39
The Cosmopolitan Lens 1: Theory 40

vi   *Contents*

The Cosmopolitan Lens 2: From the Long Take to
   Transnational Youth Cultures 45
The Cosmopolitan Lens 3: Framing the Little Space 48
Vienna 51

5   Europe 95   53

Cinema and the Real World 53
A Contemporary European Space 54
On the Train 1: Travelling around Europe 56
On the Train 2: A Story of Nineteenth-Century
   Cosmopolitanism and Nationalism 59

6   Comedy and (Lost) Youth   71

(Just) Before Sunset at the Cradle of Comedy 71
'I'm Trying to Make You Laugh' 73
Regeneration and the Masquerade 77

Bibliography   *81*
Index   *88*

Figures

3.1–3.2	Vienna after Céline and Jesse	31
3.3	Love the morning after	32
3.4	Old man with a bag at the Moses Fountain	33
3.5	In awe of the vitality of youth	34
3.6	Céline is upset at their decision to rein in desire	38
4.1	The slow pace of young love	46
4.2–4.4	Framing the little space in between … and beyond	50
4.5	Kissing outside the opera	51
5.1	Looking back at the cosmopolitanism of 'the railway age'	60
5.2–5.3	Vienna: a crucible of the old and the new	63
5.4–5.6	From 'Come Here' to Maria-Theresien-Platz	65
5.7–5.8	The Danube: European history as mise-en-scène	68
6.1–6.2	The present and the past of the couple almost cross paths in Greece	74
6.3–6.6	Looking back, moving on – the spirit of comedy	76

Series Editors' Introduction

Despite the high visibility of youth films in the global media marketplace, especially since the 1980s when Conglomerate Hollywood realized that such films were not only strong box office performers but also the starting point for ancillary sales in other media markets as well as for franchise building, academic studies that focused specifically on such films were slow to materialize. Arguably the most important factor behind academia's reluctance to engage with youth films was a (then) widespread perception within the Film and Media Studies communities that such films held little cultural value and significance, and therefore were not worthy of serious scholarly research and examination. Just like the young subjects they represented, whose interests and cultural practices have been routinely deemed transitional and transitory, so were the films that represented them perceived as fleeting and easily digestible, destined to be forgotten quickly, as soon as the next youth film arrived in cinema screens a week later.

Under these circumstances, and despite a small number of pioneering studies in the 1980s and early 1990s, the field of 'youth film studies' did not really start blossoming and attracting significant scholarly attention until the 2000s and in combination with similar developments in cognate areas such as 'girl studies.' However, because of the paucity of material in the previous decades, the majority of these new studies in the 2000s focused primarily on charting the field and therefore steered clear of long, in-depth examinations of youth films or was exemplified by edited collections that chose particular films to highlight certain issues to the detriment of others. In other words, despite providing often wonderfully rich accounts of youth cultures as these have been captured by key films, these studies could not have possibly dedicated sufficient space to engage with more than just a few key aspects of youth films.

In more recent (post-2010) years a number of academic studies started delimiting their focus and therefore providing more space for in-depth examinations of key types of youth films, such as slasher films and biker films or examining youth films in particular historical periods. From that point on, it was a matter of time for the first publications that focused exclusively on key youth films from a number of perspectives to appear (*Mamma Mia! The Movie*, *Twilight* and *Dirty Dancing* are among the first films to receive this treatment). Conceived primarily as edited collections, these studies provided a multifaceted analysis of these films, focusing on such issues as the politics of representing youth, the stylistic and narrative choices that characterise these films and the extent to which they are representative of a youth cinema, the ways these films address their audiences, the ways youth audiences engage with these films, the films' industrial location and other relevant issues.

It is within this increasingly maturing and expanding academic environment that the **Cinema and Youth Cultures** volumes arrive, aiming to consolidate existing knowledge, provide new perspectives, apply innovative methodological approaches, offer sustained and in-depth analyses of key films and therefore become the 'go to' resource for students and scholars interested in theoretically informed, authoritative accounts of youth cultures in film. As editors, we have tried to be as inclusive as possible in our selection of key examples of youth films by commissioning volumes on films that span the history of cinema, including the silent film era; that portray contemporary youth cultures as well as ones associated with particular historical periods; that represent examples of mainstream and independent cinema; that originate in American cinema and the cinemas of other nations; that attracted significant critical attention and commercial success during their initial release and that were 'rediscovered' after an unpromising initial critical reception. Together these volumes are going to advance youth film studies while also being able to offer extremely detailed examinations of films that are now considered significant contributions to cinema and our cultural life more broadly.

We hope readers will enjoy the series.

Siân Lincoln & Yannis Tzioumakis

Cinema & Youth Cultures Series Editors

Acknowledgements

Research towards this book was funded by Research Project PID2021-123836NB-I00 of the MCIN/AEI/10.13039/501100011033 and FEDER 'Una manera de hacer Europa' and by the Diputación General de Aragón (H12).
We would like to thank the editors of the series for suggesting this project, for their enthusiastic support throughout the process and for their painstaking help with the manuscript. Our gratitude goes also to Carlo Cenciarelli and Ignacio Deleyto for their help with some of the musical aspects of the analysis. We would also like to thank James MacDowell for sharing the manuscript of one of his articles before publication and, more generally, to him and Rob Stone for their extensive work on the trilogy, which, as the book shows, has served as inspiration for our own work even if we do not always see eye to eye with their views. Thanks are also due to Carolina Amaral for sharing with us her article 'Do encontró à duração: amor na trilogía *Antes do amanecer, Antes do pôr sol* e *Antes da meia-note*', before it was published.

We also thank Andrea Regueira for helping us with bibliography on Generation X and to her and the rest of the members of our research group (Manoli Ruiz, Julia Echeverría, Pablo Gómez, Andrés Bartolomé, Isabel Treviño and Andrés Buesa) for being part of a stimulating environment for our work.

Finally, we are sure that we represent a large number of scholars and fans whose lives and work were touched by the trilogy in expressing our gratitude to Julie Delpy, Ethan Hawke and Richard Linklater.

Introduction
Out of the Past

Twenty-eight years after its release in 1995, it is difficult not to situate *Before Sunrise* (Linklater) in the past. It is not only that more than a quarter of a century has passed since then and that we can now only look at the film and its cultural and cinematic impact retrospectively. It is not only that so many crucial changes have taken place around us so as to render the world it depicts and even the type of cinema it represents almost unrecognisable. It is not only that its *faux* simplicity and cool emotionality immediately suffuses contemporary spectators in nostalgia. It is also that, alongside their powerful rendition of the notion and feeling of presentness, the film and the trilogy more broadly (*Before Sunset* [Linklater 2004] and *Before Midnight* [Linklater 2013]) remain curiously past-oriented, both because of the conversations and the personalities of their protagonists and because of the complex network of references to the history of cinema and to a multitude of older films that can be found in the three instalments, and that the critics derive enormous pleasure from spotting. And it is also that within the fictional world inhabited by Céline (Julie Delpy) and Jesse (Ethan Hawke), the film, which later became the beginning of a trilogy, also became the past of two fictional characters. From the vantage point of the two protagonists of *Before Midnight*, the past to be found in *Before Sunrise* is the age of youth. Our examination of youth in the film, therefore, involves a look at the past; not only because of its release date but also because, in a parallel universe to ours, Céline and Jesse, separately or together, surely continue to ponder about the time and place they first met.

In the past quarter of a century the fascination that the film has exerted over its ever-growing fan base and in the academic community has grown exponentially. The fact that a fourth film seems more and more unlikely at this point does not seem to have diminished the love and admiration for the trilogy of many people around the world, including the Film Studies community. Critical explorations of *Before Sunrise* (and of the *Before* trilogy as a whole) abound. Some of its most famous scenes, its 'realistic' style and the intricate web of film references at the heart of the movie have been the object of much academic writing. In this sense, in looking at *Before Sunrise* in retrospect, we also, however obliquely, engage with a critical history that is as fascinating as the films themselves. While staying within the parameters of the Cinema and

DOI: 10.4324/9781003224334-1

Youth Cultures series, we have attempted to offer novel angles – to look at the film differently. But we are very much part of the same adoring community and, as academics, inevitably explain the impact of the three films in our lives in ways that ultimately rationalise what is basically a critical love story. This book is, then, both a scholarly examination of *Before Sunrise* and a statement of our sense of enchantment with its characters as they walk through life and through particular, and particularly attractive, spaces. Taking our cue from Céline and Jesse's crossing of paths when they first meet on their way to Vienna, our study is organised around a series of journeys, which to us encapsulate what is distinctive and important about the film. Opening the book's own route through the worlds inhabited by the film, Chapter 1 deals with the particular type of mobility displayed by the film and their characters, one that is steeped in the 1990s US youth cultures, associated with Generation X and the notion of the slacker. Chapter 2 explores the journey of independent cinema from the margins to the centre of the industry and, simultaneously, the journey of romantic comedy, one of the most popular genres of the 1990s, from the Hollywood mainstream towards the newly defined 'indie' cinema and the latter's focus on youth cultures and realism. This chapter also deals with the history of the film's production, reception and later life, one of whose most outstanding outcomes was the spectacular journey of director Richard Linklater from regional cinema to a cinema of transnational encounters. Chapter 3 starts the close analysis of the film, which will continue in Chapters 4 and 5. The journey described in this case is that of the characters, two emerging adults traversing the age of possibilities, through some of the decade's protocols and scripts regarding love and relationships. Chapter 4 explores the characters' cross-border journey from a cosmopolitan perspective and highlights the relevance of the characters' nationality and age in the type of transnational imagination the film deploys. Chapter 5 describes the cultural and political journey of Europe towards a utopian transnational identity as witnessed and constructed from the film's hybrid insider/outsider perspective, a journey that was continued in increasing earnest by the two sequels. Chapter 6 tells the journey of the film itself as, over the course of the following eighteen years, it became the first instalment of a much-loved trilogy which, as a whole, created an increasingly rich parallel world to that of its audiences, one with a profound comic view of life.

Our focus remains, for the most part, on *Before Sunrise*, but there is something artificial about ignoring what came after in the form of two sequels while analysing the film. The first five chapters remain largely within the confines of the 1995 movie, but Chapter 6 acknowledges the ultimate inseparability of the trilogy in the spectators' and scholars' imaginations. The film depicts an idea of youth characterised by the enjoyment of the here and now, the pleasure of being on the move and crossing borders, and the openness to the other. More obliquely, it also reveals an intense engagement with place and history. Looking back at the film from the vantage point of today, more than twenty-five years later, this book assesses the importance of *Before Sunrise* in the history of contemporary cinema, re-evaluates its critical interpretations and offers new avenues of analysis. Our study reframes the film's young romance within the context of cross-border mobilities and highlights the symbolic value of youth for the cosmopolitan imagination that is at the heart of the European project.

1 Youth Cultures in the 1990s

Strangers on a Train

June 16, 1994. A couple of twenty-somethings meet on a train in Europe. She is French and is going back to her home in Paris after visiting her grandmother in Budapest. He, a US citizen, has been travelling around Europe for a couple of weeks. His destination is now Vienna, where he will take a flight back to the US the following morning. When they get to Vienna, he suggests that she gets off the train with him so that they can spend some time together. He frames his 'admittedly insane idea' as a form of 'time travel'. He presents himself as one of those 'missed chances' the young woman's future self will reminisce about in ten (or maybe twenty) years' time when she is married and starts feeling that her marriage 'doesn't have that same energy that it used to have':

> what this really could be is a gigantic favour to both you and your future husband to find out that you are not missing out on anything. I'm just as big a loser as he is. Totally unmotivated. Totally boring. You made the right choice. And you are really happy.

The young man's *carpe diem* proposition (or maybe a conscious or unconscious desire to invest in her future happiness) strikes a chord with her and she agrees to get off the train with him. Before she sets foot on Austrian soil, she takes a second to look around, smiles to herself and quickly presses her lips together to conceal her smile. She is not aware of the implications of this narrative move for her fictional character (and for the viewers that will follow her throughout this film and the rest of the *Before* trilogy), but her face is already brimming over with joy at the potential and possibilities of this random encounter. In a different generic framework, the female character's decision to get off the train with a complete stranger could have turned nasty, tragic even. Yet, fifteen minutes into the movie, the magic space of romantic comedy (Deleyto 2009) has already started to cast its spell on the young couple. 'If I turn out to be some kind of psycho you only need to get on the next train', says the male character, a line that is dismissed as a joke by both of them. From the perspective of the spectators, it is easy to see that all the

DOI: 10.4324/9781003224334-2

stylistic devices employed by the film so far (the warm colours of the mise-en-scène, the soundtrack and the short framing distances, together with the fluid use of shot/reverse shot) are conducive to the characters' desires. At the station lobby, while looking for a locker for their luggage, they finally learn each other's names: Céline and Jesse. This unusual tardiness to disclose the characters' names (sixteen minutes into the movie) is part of the narrative's general reluctance to offer us any 'factual' information regarding the two characters. We know that Céline studies at the Sorbonne, that her parents are still married, that her father is an architect and that she has spent some time abroad both with and without her parents (which is one of the reasons why her English is so good). Regarding Jesse, we know that he has a sister, that his parents are divorced, that he took French at school and was incapable of speaking it when he went to France, and that the reason that took him to Europe was a girlfriend taking an Art Studies programme in Madrid, who broke up with him shortly after he landed in Spain. We never get to know Jesse's exact age nor the characters' surnames. We do not know what Céline is studying at the Sorbonne nor the actual status of Jesse's academic or working background/situation. None of this is for lack of conversation since dialogue is one of the features that characterises not only *Before Sunrise* but, for some critics, Richard Linklater's cinema as a whole (Deleyto 2009: 166; Stone 2018: 104–37). *Before Sunrise* is a movie about two characters getting to know and, in the process, falling in love with each other, but it is also about two characters talking about themselves, about their innermost dreams, fears, hopes and anxieties. These two drives are intrinsically intertwined since it is their talking that ignites and incites their sexual desire. Yet, Céline and Jesse's 'sexy' conversation is not the fast repartee of other romantic comedies, like those of the screwball tradition. It is, as Glen Norton puts it, 'seductive slack', in which the characters 'walk around, talk, reveal something of themselves, then cover themselves once more' (2000: 65). That, for Norton, is characteristic of what he calls the 'Gen-X genre' of the early 1990s.

'Talkin' 'bout My Generation'

The fact that this is a movie about two young characters that takes place in the early 1990s places it in the context of the decade's Generation X. A few years before Richard Linklater had directed *Slacker* (1991), the small-budget Austin-set film that gave a name to the most famous (mostly male) Gen-X type: 'the post-beatnik idler who spurned career, ambition and political activism in favour of just hanging out' (Stone 2007: 219). Linklater's debut feature is sometimes credited with having captured the *zeitgeist* of a wandering and non-committal generation, a tall order if one takes into account the regional specificity of the film and its emphasis on mainly aimless male characters. Additionally, in 1994, just one year before the release of *Before Sunrise*, Ethan Hawke had starred in *Reality Bites* (Stiller), for some 'the most polished of a bunch of mainstream attempts' to portray the ambivalences of Generation X (Roberts 2019).

Associations with that generational label are commonplace in most writing on *Before Sunrise*. For Norton, Linklater is 'Generation X film director personified' and his films 'the epitome of the Gen-X genre' because of 'their embodiment of the formula in the *text itself*, not just by the characters within' (2000: 62). *Before Sunrise* is, for him, 'the first modernist Gen-X film' (71) and 'one of the most beautifully complicated and seductive works in the short history of films by, for, and about Generation X' (72). For Christina Lee, both *Before Sunrise* and its sequel, *Before Sunset*, are 'a more grounded and tangible approach of the experience of Generation X' than Linklater's *Slacker* and *Waking Life*, which she sees as 'abstractions of social experiences' (2010: 144–5). Peter Hanson (2002), for his part, regards Linklater's *Before* films as more accurate portrayals of Generation X than *Reality Bites*, even if he considers Jesse an unusual Gen-X character:

> And even though Jesse is unmistakably a slacker with his fashionably trimmed goatee, shaggy hair, laundry-day wardrobe, and prematurely jaded attitude, he isn't limited by his generational identity. [...] Jesse is a believable, complex character who happens to belong to Generation X.
>
> (45)

For all the apparent critical consensus on the film's (and its director's) generational credentials, Hanson's quotation highlights some of the contradictions in a ready-to-use term that is sometimes more slippery and elusive than accurate and informative. The term itself has a longer history than many people think. John M. Ulrich argues in the introduction to *GenXegesis* that war photographer Robert Capa was the first to use the term in the early 1950s as the title of a project that aimed to capture, through photographs and interviews, the lives of twenty-year-olds around the world (2003: 5). In spite of its global aspirations, the project, which ended up being published in different versions in the magazines *Picture Post* and *Holiday* in 1953, 'exhibits a distinct emphasis on the experiences of western Europeans and Americans, who make up more than half of the individuals featured' (ibid.).

In 1964, Charles Hamblett and Jane Deverson's study of British youth subcultures narrowed down the scope of the term from Capa's global approach to the UK. Their book *Generation X* is an edited collection of interviews, which also includes letters and other writings received in response to a request for contributions published in *The Observer*. There is apparently no connection between Capa's use of the term and Hamblett and Deverson's, even if both pieces share the idea of representing a young identity still in the making. The young protagonists of Capa's project described themselves as apolitical and very little interested in world affairs (quoted in Whelan 1985:

278). Hamblett and Deverson, for their part, considered that what was specific about their 'generation X' is that they were the first to face 'the problem of social and scientific acceleration at the expense of biological time' (1964: 5). Yet, their study also identifies typical coming-of-age issues such as apoliticism, the rejection of parental authority and the values of mainstream society, an emphasis on the boredom of everyday life and a view of the future as uncertain.

Douglas Coupland's novel, *Generation X: Tales for an Accelerated Culture*, published in 1991, put its particular version of the term on the cultural map. The book's subtitle seems a direct reference to the process of acceleration already described by Hamblett and Deverson almost three decades earlier, even if the focus is now not on British youth in the 1960s but on three US characters in the California desert breathing dust and walking their dogs while trying to learn some truth about themselves. In a later piece (1995: 72), Coupland explained that the title and the characters from the novel came from the chapter 'The X Way Out' in Paul Fussell's book *Class: A Guide through the American Status System*, published in 1983. In Fussell's humorous analysis of the class system in the US in the 1980s, the group he refers to as 'X people' represent a 'classless class': '[t]hey occupy the one social place in the U.S.A. where the ethic of buying and selling is not all-powerful' (186). They are unprovincial, avid readers, very verbal, cynical and watch a lot of television, usually re-runs of series and television shows. They are also characterised by their comfortable and unkempt sartorial style: 'down vests, flannel shirts and hiking boots' (180). Fussell's X people have striking similarities with the 1990s slackers mentioned above, which raises doubts about the historical specificity that is usually granted to the type after 1991.

Coupland's book was published in 1991, which was also the year of the official release of Linklater's *Slacker* and of Nirvana's album *Nevermind*. The three events, which Ulrich describes as 'the political triumvirate of Coupland, Linklater and Cobain' (2003: 29), marked the beginning of Generation X as it is now generally understood in everyday parlance. This Generation X has a more classificatory urge behind it than previous uses of the term and, unlike Capa's and Hamblett and Deverson's, seems to be restricted to the US. It has come to signify the generation that came after the baby boomers. Members of this age cohort also go by the names of Baby Busters or the 13th Generation (Strauss and Howe 1991). Basically, it includes US people born between 1965 and 1980, even if the exact dates vary according to the source used, which, in strictly demographic terms, makes it a rather nebulous age group (Sternberg 2002: 89).

Yet, this use of the label is not just the result of the random convergence of three relatively small cultural events happening in 1991: Coupland's small 1991 printing of the book, for example, had no publicity and received almost no reviews (Coupland 1995: 72). In her book *Marketing to Generation X* (1995), marketing executive Karen Ritchie recounts having used the word for the first time in an American Magazine Conference in Bermuda in 1992. She had read Coupland's book ('I didn't get it, but I liked the name') and used the term to tell the assembled publishers that it was time they started targeting the generation that came after the Boomers: 'Generation X... the purple-haired people... Your kids, [...] and mine' (1995: 6–8). Ritchie was not the first to notice the, by-then, invisibility of the generation that came after the Boomers, even if she may have been the first to call them Generation X. A piece by Gross and Scott published in *Time* on July 16, 1990, uses the term 'neglected generation' to refer to the same age cohort: 'the twentysomething generation, those 48 million young Americans ages 18 through 29 who fall between the famous baby boomers and the boomlet of children the baby boomers are producing'. According to independent film producer John Pierson, Gross and Scott's eight-page cover story was one of the press clippings Linklater sent to him when he was trying to find a distributor for *Slacker* (2014: 187). In his letter to Pierson, Linklater described the twentysomething generation that he saw as a potential niche for his movie with the following words: 'urban, educated (anyone who made it past their sophomore year in college), and one that typically reads up on movies before they see them' (quoted in Savlov 2011).

According to Ritchie, nothing had prepared her for the 'barrage of attention that followed' (1995: 8). Immediately after the Bermuda conference, she was invited by media groups and private companies to speak to them about Generation X, which soon became 'the phrase that launched a thousand magazine articles' (Bernstein, quoted in Sternberg 2002: 86). A stereotypical portrait of the newly discovered US age cohort soon followed: they were constructed as bored, frustrated, cynical, media savvy, apathetic, over-educated and under-employed, among other epithets. They were usually described in opposition to the baby boomers, and monikers such as slackers, whiners or the MTV generation were thrown into the discursive bag (Ortner 1998: 419). According to demographic data, the Generation X cohort was the most ethnically diverse generation to date. And yet, race was virtually absent in most of the discourses about Generation X (420).

The shortcomings of this psychographic of GenXers were also voiced by some. Bob Guccione Jr., at the time editor and publisher of the music magazine *SPIN*, wrote in 1993 that the stereotypical description of Generation X was a marketing campaign orchestrated by Boomers to make young people less desirable to employers:

> Young people are essentially no different today than they have ever been. Only the conditions are different, as they always were. Young people are simply young and must go through what we people who are a little older had to go through: the process of learning about life. One would hope that older people would be grateful for their acquired wisdom and not resentful of younger people.
>
> (1993)

Coupland (1995: 72) complained that advertising executives and journalists were using the characters he had created to represent a whole generation; something that the author, a Canadian living in Montreal at the time, felt very uncomfortable with. As some started to claim, the discourse on Generation X was a misrepresentation (Haworth 1997), a media creation injected into the body of youth through the media (Sternberg 2002: 88).

Maybe, as some have claimed, Generation X never actually existed beyond the shifting discourses about it (Ortner 1998: 416), but those discourses were real enough not only to name later generations in a similar way (Generation Y, Z and Alpha) but also to prompt some people to postulate themselves as members of the generation. In *The Generation X Reader*, Douglas Rushkoff describes Generation X as a 'life philosophy designed to help us cope with the increasingly and disorientingly rapid deflation of our society, both financially and culturally' (1994: 6).

As emerges from this short history of the term (which has glossed over some well-known iterations as the name of Billy Idol's band from 1976 to 1981, apparently inspired by Hamblett and Deverson's book), what its different uses have in common is that they refer to young people in their twenties, the X becoming the way to represent a young identity in the making. When looked at closely, the GenXers of the 1950s, 1960s and 1990s also seem to have in common their apoliticism, their little interest in the world outside their most immediate sphere, a prevailing feeling of boredom and a rejection of most forms of authority. In this sense, what seems to unite them all is that they are navigating what Jeffrey Arnett has called 'emerging adulthood', a process that, he argues, at least in the US, became gradually longer in the second half of the twentieth century as a result of various socio-historical changes (2004).

Given the vagueness, contradictions and even arbitrariness of the term 'Generation X', one might be tempted to discard it altogether, particularly as a context to a film (and later a trilogy) that takes place in Europe and in which one half of the couple is European. In this book, we will not be describing either Céline or Jesse as 'Xers' and yet we feel that it is important to keep in sight the cultural background in which the film originates and the discursive association of its director and, specifically, the film with this label. Part of the relevance of *Before Sunrise* as a youth culture film is, as we will develop further in Chapter 2, the nature of its transition from a culturally and historically specific US context to a transnational and, specifically, trans-European one. In order to understand the impact of this journey, it is crucial to be familiar with the context in which it begins: that of a director who, through this film and others, became, as we have pointed out, a flagpole for a generation in his country and ended up delivering a canvas of historical developments in Europe in the course of three decades. While 'Generation X' may be of limited use to explain the cultural realities of the film that *Before Sunrise* became, it does condense the historical ferment from which it originated. On the other hand, a parallel concept, which in the case of Linklater, was always very close to Generation X, contains greater explicatory potential for our understanding of the film. That is the term 'slacker'.

Cut Them Some Slack

'He will turn this place into a den of slack'. These are the words with which Lelaina Pierce (Wynona Ryder) resentfully criticises the fact that her roommate has invited their common friend Troy (Ethan Hawke) to crash on their couch for a couple of weeks in the 1994 movie *Reality Bites*. Lelaina, class valedictorian and aspiring documentary filmmaker, cannot stand what she refers to as her friend's mastery 'at the art of time suckage'. The popularity of the term 'slacker' at the time was such that even then-US president Bill Clinton used it in a speech at UCLA on May 20, 1994:

> Americans of my generation have been bombarded by images on television shows, and even one book, about the so-called Generation X filled with cynics and slackers. Well, what I have seen today is not a generation of slackers, but a generation of seekers.

As has been sufficiently argued, Linklater did not coin the word 'slacker'. Its origins can be traced back to the Latin word *laxus*, meaning loose, which is also the root of the word 'relax'. Apparently, it was used mainly in nautical contexts prior to World War I, when the term 'slacker' started to be used as a derogatory word for somebody who engaged in any kind of unpatriotic behaviour. Soon it became a synonym for 'draft dodger', as can be seen in the titles of silent films such as *The Slacker* (Cabanne 1917), *The Slacker's Heart* (Ireland 1917) and *Mrs. Slacker* (Henley 1918), among others. Slacker lists were printed in newspapers and slacker raids were conducted in the cities. After World War I, the term lost some of its specificity and started to be used to refer to somebody who evades work or a specific duty (Safire 1994; Kluft 2014). Yet, what Linklater can take credit for is putting the word on the map in its contemporary sense as a term to describe a (usually young) person, with plenty of time on their hands, that puts that time to a use that is not always the socially sanctioned one. In line with the characters (and the narrative structure) of Linklater's film, the term 'lazy drifters' has also become synonymous with slackers. Yet, Linklater has a different way of understanding the type as 'people who are ultimately being responsible to themselves and not wasting their time in a realm of activity that has nothing to do with who they are or what they might ultimately be striving for' (Linklater 2020).

For Rob Stone, who minutely describes the historical and geographical context (Austin in the 1980s) in which *Slacker* developed, the slacking ethos is a constant in Linklater's filmography, from *It's Impossible to Learn to Plow by Reading Books* (1988) to *Boyhood* (2014). For Stone, Linklater's slack has clear links with European culture: he underlines its existential and

Marxist undercurrents, the explicit connection to the French *nouvelle vague*, particularly Jean-Luc Godard's *À bout de souffle* (1960), Robert Bresson's *L'argent* (1983) and the films of Eric Rohmer, to James Joyce's *Ulysses* and to Guy Debord's concept of *dérive*, among other influences. The stream of consciousness of James Joyce's *Ulysses* is, for Stone, a clear model for *Before Sunrise* (2007: 225), a kind of narrative of slacking *avant la lettre*, a connection underlined in *Before Sunrise*, whose action takes place on Bloomsday (and also in *Before Sunset*, which starts at the Shakespeare and Company bookstore, where *Ulysses* was first published in 1922) (27–29). Stone quotes from Debord's summary of his own concept:

> In a *dérive* one or more persons during a certain period drop their usual motives for movement and action, their relations, their work and leisure activities, and let themselves be drawn by the attractions of the terrain and the encounters they find there
>
> (2007: 50).

Linklater's and Stone's redefinitions of the term attempt to 'rescue' it from the connotations of laziness that are at the heart of the Generation X discourse described above, or as Stone puts it, 'the widely misunderstood slacker philosophy' (2007: 6). They are not alone in the endeavour. Rachel J. Heiman (2001) reads the Gen-X slacker type as a 'critique of the Fordist idea of productivity', one that expected workers to be diligent and committed to their jobs and also restrained and rational when it came to consumption and leisure (276). Similar ideas of resistance (and eventual resignation) to some of the dynamics of neoliberal capitalism are at the heart of Andrew Kopkind's (1992) and Mark John Isola's (2013) analyses of the slacker figure. Henry A. Giroux refers to his students' description of the slacker as a young person who is privileged enough to have time to think, travel and relax for a while before they make 'some important decisions about their lives' (1996: 39). As a deliberate refusal to sell out, a critique of a specific work ethic or a transitory stage to find one's identity and think about the future, what these readings have in common is the boundaries of the category, mainly restricted to white and usually college-educated twenty-somethings: 'I'd like to be a slacker, but my family would kick my ass. A poor Mexican worrying about esoteric emotions like angst? Get a job, *mijo*' (Lalo López, quoted in Ritchie, 1995: 59). Eliot Tretter has explored the links between the Austin slacker, a type that, he argues, is unmistakably raced and classed, and the gentrification of Austin since the 1990s. As he puts it, 'Richard Linklater's figure of the slacker was not a victim of a transforming city but rather a willing participant in a sociocultural transformation' that aimed to remove non-white people from certain areas of the city (2020).

It seems that the ability to be a slacker is a privilege only some can afford, as emerges from the representations of the type in the 'slacker cycle' of the early 1990s (Kehr 1993). *Singles*, Cameron Crowe's 1992 movie about six single white friends living in Seattle in the early 1990s, is one of the earliest representations of the type. Crowe's movie replaces the snake-like narrative structure (*à la* Max Ophüls's *La Ronde* [1950]) of *Slacker* with an episodic narrative pattern in which four of the film's characters take turns to act as direct internal narrators. Some of them have typical slacker jobs: Janet (Bridget Fonda) is a waitress and Cliff (Matt Dillon) moonlights as a waiter and a delivery guy while struggling to make it in the burgeoning grunge music scene. Even those characters with more career-oriented jobs – Steve (Campbell Scott) works at the Seattle Department of Transportation and Linda (Kyra Sedgwick) in an Environmental Organisation – have a lot of time on their hands which, in their case, is used to slack with their friends and discuss dating and sexual protocols, among other issues. This seems to be one of the favourite pastimes of white twenty-somethings in 1990s films like *Beautiful Girls* (Demme 1996), *Clerks* (Smith 1994), *Bodies, Rest and Motion* (Steinberg 1993), *Kicking and Screaming* (Baumbach 1995), *Walking and Talking* (Holofcener 1996) and *Chasing Amy* (Smith 1997), as well as *The Brothers McMullen* (1995) and *She's the One* (1996), both directed by Edward Burns, in which the group of friends is replaced by family members. As quintessential slacker Troy puts it to his friend Lelaina in *Reality Bites*: 'This is all we need: a couple of smokes, a cup of coffee and a little bit of conversation'. Slacking at the coffee house with a group of friends is also the favourite pastime of the characters in the audio-visual text that became the epitome of emerging white adulthood in the early 1990s: the sitcom *Friends* (NBC 1994–2004).

Like Troy and the six famous sitcom friends, the two protagonists of *Before Sunrise* seem quite content with several cups of coffee (or beers) and a little bit (or a lot of) of conversation. Like most characters in the films mentioned above, they also voice typical slacker concerns: as Céline says, they feel that, unlike their parents' generation, they have nothing to rebel against; or, as Jesse puts it, he resents his Boomer parents because he always felt he was 'crashing the big party'. What sets Jesse and Céline apart from most of them is their willingness to engage in cross-border mobility. As we find out fifty-five minutes into the plot of *Before Sunrise*, Jesse saved up all his money to fly to Madrid and spend the summer with his girlfriend. Faced with a similar situation, Grover (Josh Hamilton) in *Kicking and Screaming* is unsupportive of his girlfriend's decision to move to Prague and enrol in a postgraduate writing programme. He resorts to worn-out cliches about the country he keeps referring to as Czechoslovakia since, as he tells his father, he has not had much time to read the press lately. As he puts it: 'I haven't "been to Prague" been to Prague but I know that thing, that "Stop shaving your armpits, read *The Unbearable Lightness of Being*, date a sculptor, now I know how bad American coffee is thing"'. Even if he makes the on-the-spot decision to travel to Prague near the end of the film, he finds himself at the airport without a passport and, therefore, unable to buy a ticket. As the film's ending makes clear, Grover's world is bound to remain as parochial and homogenous in terms of nationality, race and class as the university campus where he and his male friends insist on staying, even after graduation. Similarly, Francis, Edward Burns's character in *She's the One*, is unable to fathom the reasons why his recent wife may want to move to Paris ('the place where they hate Americans') to do her PhD. Unlike these slackers, Jesse and Céline are articulations of a very specific kind of cosmopolitan disposition and seem to feel at home in the world.

It can be surmised, therefore, that in *Before Sunrise*, the slacker ethos described by Linklater himself, Rob Stone, and others crosses the border. Given the European inspiration traced by Stone, it may have seemed paradoxical that the concerns of cinematic slackers in the 1990s, including those of the director himself in *Slacker*, should have been so parochial. As we will discuss in detail in the next chapter, the original inspiration for the story of *Before Sunrise* was just as locally minded: the young man and woman are two Americans meeting by chance at the train station in San Antonio, Texas. But then Linklater, whose name was becoming familiar among second-wave 'independent US directors' travelled to Austria and the story took a U-turn. Metaphorically, slack returned to Europe and, with the change of space, a new set of concerns arose. What remained was the focus on youth and the exploration of the hopes, fantasies, anxieties and frustrations of twentysomething women and men at the turn of the century. As the film morphed in the course of its transatlantic journey, those experiences became fused with the different concerns of young European people in the context of a young, or rejuvenated, Europe. In more than one way, the rest is history. That history is the main point of interest of this book.

2 Indie, Comic and Transnational

The Production of *Before Sunrise* in Context

Linklater and the Journey of Indie Cinema in the 1990s

Richard Linklater has been associated with contemporary US independent cinema ever since the initial impact of *Slacker* (1991). He was one of the most representative directors of what we might call the second wave of the independent film movement in the 1990s. Emmanuel Levy includes him, along with Quentin Tarantino, Robert Rodriguez, Edward Burns and others, under the label 'heroes of the new indie cinema' (1999: 15–19). The director's approach to financing his film projects – 'patchwork funding', as Stone defines it (2018: 115) – epitomises, in more than one sense, the variety of opportunities offered by the industry in the 1990s, as well as its risks and vagaries, and independent cinema's well-known uneasy relationship with industrial considerations (San Filippo 2015: 55; Tzioumakis 2017: 227–46; Stone 2018: 13–14).

In terms of the industrial framework, specialists' appraisals have evolved from Levy's nuanced double conception of independent cinema as either a) including any US films financed outside Hollywood, or b) films with a fresh perspective and a personal vision (1999: 3) to Tzioumakis's shedding of the provenance of finance as part of the equation altogether. For the latter, if we compare those films produced or distributed by earlier independent companies with those produced or distributed by the majors' specialty divisions, it is difficult to argue that some are more or less independent than others (2017: 243). It is the *discourse* of independence that matters, that is, the self-fashioning of the companies, the filmmakers and the films themselves as offering 'independence of vision' (11). Ultimately, as San Filippo argues for the cinema of the twenty-first century, while the label 'independent' has gone a long way towards explaining what was distinctive about US cinema from the mid-1970s to the 2000s, and although it continues to enjoy a high degree of critical and industrial valency, the binary 'Hollywood vs indie' fails to capture the industrial and artistic complexity of contemporary cinema (2015: 53). Still, there is little doubt about the success and longevity of the label, even as the constellation of meanings around it remains less than clear. Indie films, as independents started to be called when they became institutionally indistinguishable from the mainstream (Tzioumakis 2017: 227, 243), did not,

DOI: 10.4324/9781003224334-3

after all, just prove financially viable starting in the 1980s, they also changed the face of cinema around the turn of the century.

San Filippo offers her insight as part of the introduction to her study of the *Before* trilogy. Her blurring of the boundaries between mainstream and independence makes particular good sense in the context of Linklater's *oeuvre* as a whole, for, while the label continues to be attached to his figure and his filmmaking practices, his relationship to the industry illustrates his flexibility of approach with each new project. The director himself confesses that he would like to have been Vincente Minnelli or Howard Hawks, who worked for the studios while secretly making their own films (Speed, quoted in Stone 2018: 115). For him, it has been less a matter of maintaining financial independence from the centre of the industry than of finding the best way to get his projects underway. While his first feature film, *It's Impossible to Learn to Plow by Reading Books*, was completely self-financed – it cost a total of $3,000 – and was never distributed, for his breakthrough *Slacker*, he gathered the meagre budget of $23,000 from loans and grants. While being screened at the Dobie Theater in Austin, it attracted the interest of Orion Classics, which committed a small amount of $150,000 to its completion and distribution, making it ready for Sundance, where it reached the necessary visibility (Macor 2010: 104–10). By contrast, his next project, *Dazed and Confused* (1993), came into existence through a production deal with Universal. But it was *Before Sunrise* that first exhibited Linklater's patchwork funding practice and the elasticity of the line separating independent from mainstream. For this film, he struck a 'hands-off' deal between Detour Productions, his own production company, and Castle Rock, after one of the latter's owners, Martin Shafer, read the script. Founded in 1987 by, among others, Shafer and director Rob Reiner, Castle Rock was one of the independent companies that flourished in the 1980s, thanks to the backing of the major Columbia Pictures and Nelson Entertainment. When the venture ceased to be profitable for Columbia, Castle Rock was sold to Warner Bros., thus joining the then swelling list of independent companies that either underwent corporate takeovers or struck distribution contracts with the majors (Tzioumakis 2017: 224; Stone 2018: 13). Thus, Castle Rock became an example of an independent company that was never truly independent and continued to enjoy a comparable degree of independence after it was absorbed by a major.

The takeover by Warner Bros. caught *Before Sunrise* in the middle of production: when Linklater made his deal with Castle Rock, Columbia was still part of the equation and, as such, had secured theatrical distribution rights. By the time the film went into distribution, Castle Rock had become a subsidiary of Warner Bros. Thus, Linklater's movie was both first-hand witness *and* subject of the general trajectory of US independent cinema in the 1990s and its transition towards incorporation in the Hollywood industry and the larger entertainment conglomerates, while remaining an artistic, cultural and industrial force to reckon with. Throughout the film's production, his hands-off deal ensured Linklater had control of the $2.5m budget and, therefore, a high degree of independence that did not change with the takeover. At the same time, the film had moved from the earlier films' 'tenuous modes of financing, filming and distribution' to 'the industry's terra firma' (San Filippo 2015: 54).

A Philadelphia Story

The second type of transition that *Before Sunrise* was part of originates in the event in the director's personal life that first inspired him to make the film: 'a very fun evening in Philadelphia', which he spent with a woman in 1989 while he was visiting his sister (Stone 2018: 118–19; Spencer 2020). The two walked around the city for hours and then parted ways. During their time together, Linklater conceived and even mentioned to the woman the possibility of making a film out of their experience: 'I want to make a film about this. Just this feeling' (quoted in Spencer 2020). Years later, Linklater found out that the woman, Amy Lehrhaupt, had died in a motorbike accident in 1994 (and therefore never saw the film). *Before Midnight* would be dedicated to her. The 'feeling' that Linklater wanted to capture in his film was apparently very different from the concerns of his first three movies, even if it also had elements in common with them: the solo train journey of the protagonist of *It's Impossible* …, the conversations on radically miscellaneous topics involving one hundred Austinites as they cross paths in Austin in *Slacker*, and the more or less mundane events of the last day of school among a group of senior and junior high school students in the mid-1970s in *Dazed and Confused*. Neither *It's Impossible* ... nor *Slacker* paid attention to any aspect of the internal life or emotional attachments of the characters onscreen. Although a very different film, *Dazed and Confused* also steered away from 'feelings'. In that film such tentative heterosexual pairings as began to materialise towards the end of the narrative played a very secondary role in the general depiction of the last day of school and remained underdeveloped.

The Philadelphia encounter changed all this: it became the basis for a film and then two sequels about attraction, desire, romance and heterosexual love, a field of experience that was then new for Linklater but one in which *Before Sunrise* and the trilogy would leave a lasting mark in cinema history. Simultaneously, as argued in Chapter 1, the film became one of the most representative Generation X films. The 'slacker philosophy' (Stone 2018: 6) that Linklater had depicted in his earlier films would now become attached to the examination of the intimate protocols of not one but, with the passing of years and release of the sequels, several generations.

With the exception of *sex, lies, and videotape* (Soderbergh 1989) and a few other films, independent cinema had not been particularly concerned with the exploration of love and desire among the young since its return to visibility in the late 1970s. But *Before Sunrise* did not happen in a cinematic vacuum: it appeared at a time when romantic comedy had become one of the most popular genres in Hollywood. Traditionally a genre characterised by peaks followed by periods of dearth and near-disappearance, romcom had re-emerged in the late 1970s with a small group of films, especially Woody Allen's *Annie Hall* (1977) and *Manhattan* (1979), which Frank Krutnik termed 'nervous romances' (1990: 57), and then gradually risen in visibility in the mid-1980s through more mainstream films like *Splash!* (Howard 1984), *Romancing the Stone* (Zemeckis 1985), *Something Wild* (Demme 1986), *Working Girl* (Nichols 1988) and, especially, *When Harry Met Sally ...* (Reiner 1989) and *Pretty Woman* (Marshall 1990). The last two titles in particular ushered in a golden decade for the genre, dominated by stars like Julia Roberts, Meg Ryan, Tom Hanks, Sandra Bullock, Andie MacDowell and Hugh Grant, among others. For the critical establishment, however, the connection between Linklater and the romcom was counterintuitive. If anything, independent cinema was seen as a reaction against the earnest and routine genericity that romantic comedy embodied, a reaction that could take the form of parody à la Coen Brothers and, later, Wes Anderson, or of a form of realism envisaged as the opposite from the conventionality of the mainstream. For Geoff King, for example, prominent features of independent cinema included the departure from the conventions of classical Hollywood (2005: 59), its anti-genericity (167) and its impression of authenticity (107). At the opposite end of the spectrum, the term conventionality included reliance on generic conventions and conservative values.

This association of romantic comedy with ideological conservatism and mainstream predictability has been long-standing and difficult to shake (Deleyto 2009: 24–26) and remains in good health both in the critical and academic institutions. As Tamar Jeffers McDonald emphatically puts it, 'romantic comedy is, arguably, the lowest of the low' (2007: 7). In the 1990s, as the popularity of the genre continued to grow, with films like *Sleepless in Seattle* (Ephron 1993), *While You Were Sleeping* (Turteltaub 1995), *You've Got Mail* (Ephron 1998) and *Notting Hill* (Michell 1999) dominating the screens, the genre's prestige remained low. This summary dismissal of the genre both on artistic and ideological grounds exonerated the critics from carrying out any examination of the reasons why its stories garnered such a strong appeal at that moment in time, particularly among female spectators, and of the ways in which they may have been speaking to important parts of contemporary experience. The same critical discourse was also adopted by independent cinema in the early 1990s, even as the companies, films and directors themselves drew closer to the centre of the industry. This was also the case for *Before Sunrise*.

Erasing Romcom

From the beginning the film was described, not least by Linklater himself, as a response to the success of the romantic comedy in Hollywood and as a more ambitious alternative to those films' artificiality and superficiality (see, for a short list of examples, MacDowell 2021a: 63, note 2). At Castle Rock, Martin Shafer liked the script because the story 'was so different from the so-called romantic comedies of the time, which were often very contrived, and it had such a naturalistic feel to it' (quoted in Spencer 2020). A formal feature that the new film shared with both *Slacker* and *Dazed and Confused* was its spatial and temporal restrictions, events developing in the course of one day in a single location. In *Before Sunrise*, the relationship between Céline and Jesse is structured around a series of dialogue exchanges that take place as the pair approach Vienna by train and then walk around the city for a few hours until it is time for Jesse to catch a flight back to the US and for Céline to continue her journey back to Paris. This format crucially contributed to the film's impression of realism and not only separated it from the mainstream (especially, as Shafer suggests, romantic comedy), but actively shaped it as an alternative to the latter genre. Even as the film became part of Hollywood in industrial terms, it was perceived, both in the critical discourse and in the discourse of independence, as a reaction *to* Hollywood.

The film raised academic interest soon. Robin Wood set the pace in an article that considered *Sunrise* one of the most important films of the decade, not only because of its articulation of effective gender equality in the narrative, but also because of its realism, with the usual distinction between 'being' and 'acting' merging in the film's central performances and the story's realistic acknowledgement of uncertainty, precariousness, and the transience of feelings (1998: 321, 323). As opposed to the mainstream romcoms, the added value of the film resided in the depiction of 'the slack, random, seductive moments of life' (Norton 2000: 66), a randomness that the film reproduces in its very form (72). Few seemed interested, as MacDowell argued much later for the trilogy, in its obvious genericity, both in terms of romantic comedy and melodrama (2021a: 47, 49–51). Neither did they seem to appreciate the deployment of 'old' generic conventions on the part of the film and its sequels, even if, as will be argued in Chapter 3, the film's connections with well-known romantic films such as *Love Affair* (McCarey 1939) and *An Affair to Remember* (McCarey 1957) are more than obvious. In the dominant critical view of the film we are describing, on the one hand, generic convention and realism are mutually exclusive notions, as if realism, cinematic or otherwise, were not also based on a set of, often very rigid, conventions, and as if realism and genre could never appear together. On the other hand, it appears as though it is only through realism, and not genericity, that movies can offer important insights into human nature, in this case, the view of life encapsulated in the notion of slack.

Not that realism is only about 'slice of life' stories. As argued in Chapter 1, Rob Stone, for instance, relates 'slacker philosophy' to a panoply of cinematic and philosophical references, including the *nouvelle vague*, Gilles Deleuze, Guy Debord and, especially, Henri Bergson's theory of time as always in flux, in transition, in process: 'time is what is happening, and more than that, it is what causes everything to happen' (2013: 76). Stone offers the most thorough scrutiny of the importance of temporality (living in the moment and death in *Sunrise* and in the two sequels) and persuasively links them with the film's narrative construction and its use of formal strategies. This approach relates Linklater not only to European cinema history, particularly the *nouvelle vague*, but also to high cultural traditions. In his conversation with David T. Johnson, included in the Criterion Blu-ray edition of the trilogy, Stone laments the association of the films with romantic comedy and, in the second edition of his book on the director, is relieved that *Midnight* 'rescues the *Before* trilogy from categorization as romantic comedy' (2018: 136). The implication is that this generic association is incompatible with the complex exploration of temporality and other issues that the films invite. In sum, realism can channel sophisticated art and complex views of life. Genres, particularly romantic comedy, cannot.

A narrative has, therefore, crystallised around *Before Sunrise* and the trilogy whereby the generic conventions of romantic comedy and realism are mutually exclusive, and the film's use of realism is partly a way to dissociate itself from and critique the generic mainstream. Realism, or the 'truthful' reproduction of reality and real people's experiences, are an antidote to the conventional fantasies offered by the genre. Yet, romantic comedy may be seen differently. As Deleyto has argued for *Before Sunset*, it is through the use of the codes and conventions of realism that the film makes its contribution to the genre. While not being 'real', romantic comedy uses generic devices to comment on and reflect upon the boundaries within which real people of a given period interact in intimate relationships. It may be argued that realism, after all also a set of historically specific conventions, mediates the worlds it represents as much as (other) genres. What is important is what those artistic mediations may tell us about the world (2009: 159–61). For San Filippo, in fact, the genre's key attribute in the following years was precisely the impulse to couple romcom and realism (2021: 5). There is nothing in *Before Sunrise* that differs significantly from this impulse. This ability to morph, intersect and adapt to social changes in intimate protocols is nothing new in the history of the genre. In other words, rather than a realistic alternative to romantic comedy, *Before Sunrise* became an early instance of the genre's turn to realism.

In fact, in recent times, changes in the genre have continued to occur across the spectrum, and were indeed occurring in the indie 'confessional comedies' (Levy 1999: 273) which *Before Sunrise* crucially contributed to inaugurate. More specifically, the template established by the film – which both Deleyto (2009: 163) and Stone (2018: 104) have described as 'walking and talking' after Nicole Holofcener's indie romcom of the following year, *Walking and Talking* – may be discerned in many instances of the genre in the following two decades. This is the case, for example, of Holofcener's subsequent *Lovely & Amazing* (2001), *Friends with Money* (2006) and *Enough Said* (2013), among others, and of Edward Burns's own confessional comedies such as

The Brothers McMullen, Sidewalks of New York (2001) and *The Groomsmen* (2006). It is also the case of a long list of later films, including non-US productions, such as *In Search of a Midnight Kiss* (Holdridge 2007), *500 Days of Summer* (Webb 2009), *Monsters* (Edwards 2010) and *Already Tomorrow in Hong Kong* (Ting 2015), among many others. As Oria has argued, when the romcom genre began to flag in the mainstream in the course of the first two decades of the twenty-first century, it continued to develop precisely within the realm of indie comedy, as well as in the television series produced first by the traditional channels and then, increasingly, by the streaming platforms (Oria 2018 and 2020; Alsop 2021: 219–20). The new iterations of the genre and the transformations it underwent during this time can, therefore, be traced back directly to the indie comedies of the 1990s, prominent among which was *Before Sunrise*.

Rather than as a realist film that rejects genericity, we would like to describe *Before Sunrise* as a realistic indie romantic comedy about young adults with philosophical and classical aspirations in its interest, through both cinematic form and dialogues, in the connections between love, temporality and death. In sum, *Before Sunrise* proved crucial in the genre's survival: through it and the films that followed it, romantic comedy incorporated many of the tropes of cinematic realism.

Gender, Desire and Dialogue

One of the most interesting and perhaps momentous changes of twenty-first century romantic comedy has been, as San Filippo contends, the relative decoupling of the genre from the compulsory centrality of the couple in narrativisations of contemporary desire (2021). While this development is evidently a translation into generic form of recent intimate protocols, it arguably diluted one of the dimensions of romcom that separates it from other classical genres, say, the western, the gangster or the adventure film, and indeed from most classical narrative forms, including the epic poem and the tragedy. Unlike all the above, romcom affords spectators a double perspective. In a patriarchal regime of representation like the Hollywood of the twentieth century, comedies of heterosexual desire constituted an exception in that they afforded unusual visibility and prominence to the female character's point of view (Lent 1995) even if individual instances sometimes disappointed. An avowed cinephile, Linklater seemed particularly aware of this potential of the genre, or at least of stories of heterosexual desire in general, while he was preparing for the film. Thinking perhaps of the best examples of screwball comedy, he was concerned with the lack of gender balance and the absence of the female point of view in his earlier feature films. He knew that his new film needed to be framed differently. For this reason, he asked Kim Krizan, an actor who had appeared in *Slacker* and *Dazed and Confused* and had no film writing experience, to co-write a script based on his 'Philadelphia story' (Spencer 2020). After finishing *Dazed and Confused* in the spring of 1993, Krizan and Linklater spent eleven days brainstorming: 'we each had our little notebooks and we would tell stories. It was sort of like a relationship boot camp' (Krizan, quoted in Macor 2010: 190). The resulting script incorporated the desired double perspective even though Krizan does not appear to have been entirely happy with the result: 'he'd have the guy talk, talk, talk and the girl going, "Uh huh. Uh huh". I would try to have the girl talk. But ultimately, it was his computer' (quoted in ibid.).

Linklater had warned Krizan beforehand that their script would be only a blueprint, to be developed later with the actors. For one thing, in the original script, the story was set in San Antonio, Texas, where there was a suitable train station, and the two characters were, as in the Philadelphia story, from the US (Pierson 2014: 197; Spencer 2020). But then Linklater took *Dazed and Confused* to the film festival in Vienna and, while in the Austrian capital, he learned that he could get funding from the EU if he shot his film there (Spencer 2020). The $2.5m deal with Castle Rock may have also warmed the director to the idea of moving beyond the regional cinema with which his early career had been associated (Stone 2018: 9–16).

Next came the casting process. According to Spencer, it took more than six months to cast the film; according to Macor, the best part of nine (Spencer 2020; Macor 2010: 189). During this time, actors as varied as Robin Wright, Lily Taylor, Sadie Frost (Macor 2010: 189), Gwyneth Paltrow and Jennifer Aniston (casting director Judy Henderson, quoted in Spencer 2020) auditioned for the part of Céline (although the character had no name yet at the time) in Los Angeles, but Julie Delpy seems to have been at the top of the list from the very beginning. The fact that she was European appears to have been a factor. As for the character of Jesse, Ethan Hawke spent a long evening discussing the film with Linklater in New York. When he was sent the script, he assumed that he was being offered the part. Later on, he learned from his agent that he was only being asked to audition. Other actors considered for the part were British David Thewlis and French Michael Vartan (Macor 2010: 189). Linklater says that during the casting process it was always clear that one member of the couple would be European, the other American. According to casting director Judy Henderson, in the end there were four candidates: Hawke, Delpy, Frost and Vartan. 'You could almost toss a coin' (Spencer 2020). A deciding factor appears to have been Linklater's initial decision to have two creative partners. As he had warned Krizan, he wanted the actors to participate in the writing of the story and he found that both Hawke and Delpy fitted this profile (ibid.). In the weeks prior to the shoot, already in Vienna, the three continued to revise the script. By this time, the story of a young man and a young woman, both from the US, who met in San Antonio had turned into a story in which two young people, he from the US, she from France, meet on a train and spend a few hours together in Vienna before parting ways again.

The story that had originated in a lengthy real-life conversation in Philadelphia, was shaped into a string of dialogues based on the lengthy conversations between Linklater and Krizan, and was gradually adapted to the personalities, interests and experiences of the actors. The resultant collaboration was the basis, first, for the film and then, for the other two instalments of the trilogy. In due course, it became the template for one of the dominant forms of the genre in the twenty-first century. For Stone, the film is emblematic of the dialogic and dialogue-driven cinema of Linklater – a film that was 'always about the process of its own making' (2013: 119). The realist film was, therefore, also an exercise in self-reflexivity, not only about the director's interests but also about the shape that the new romantic comedy was to take. As may have happened in the course of the Philadelphia encounter, the lovers ignite and express their desire for each other through a constant exchange of anecdotes, stories of their past, discussions about the passing of time and death, plans and projects, philosophical speculations and verbal exchanges on a series of miscellaneous issues. Throughout the trilogy, with one or two exceptions, they never seem to be short of topics of conversation. This may be because in the filmmakers' minds (including here Linklater, Krizan, Delpy and Hawke), lively, intense, intelligent conversation is erotic and desire can be naturally channelled through it (Deleyto 2009: 163–164). It may be that, with *Before Sunrise* providing the template, the new romantic comedy was beginning to sense the crisis of traditional forms of romantic love and found in the dialogue-based narrative a viable alternative, one that chimed in with new ways for young people to relate to one another. However we wish to phrase it, the intuition that the Philadelphia story might be turned into a film in which, within its own temporal boundaries, little happened in terms of plot proved attuned to the experiences of GenXers and slackers. And not only those groups: it also appealed to many other young people around the world in ways that the contemporary mainstream romcoms did not, even though they were enjoying considerable success on the global screens. Or it may be that the main attraction of the story did not primarily reside in the lively conversation or the budding desire but, rather, in the apparently everyday yet utopian sight of two young people from different countries meeting by chance on a train and engaging in a relaxed and unemphatic way within the enhanced transnational realities of 1990s Europe.

Coming to Europe

Twenty-eight years and two sequels later, the relationship between Jesse and Céline would be unimaginable with other actors and other settings or without the constant walking and talking. As the trilogy developed, the central relationship would also become inconceivable without the passing of years and decades both in the lives of the characters and of its increasingly die-hard fans and in the history of the world around them; a history that, in the films' characteristically understated way, shaped their lives apart and together. The film premiered at the Sundance Festival on January 19, 1995 and was released in cinemas a week later. It made around $5.5m in the US and Canada and a similar figure in the rest of the world. The budget for *Before Sunset* was very similar at $2.7m and the domestic gross practically the same at $5.8m and, at slightly over $10m, almost twice as much globally, with *Before Midnight* costing slightly over $8m and taking a total of just under $21m globally (source: Box Office Mojo). None of them lost money but neither were they particularly successful. The films became the 'Lowest Grossing Trilogy', according to San Filippo (2015: 55). Yet, as San Filippo describes in her account of her personal relationship with the trilogy, first *Sunrise* and then the two sequels developed a strong fan base. For this writer, the history of the reception of the movies reflects the evolution of indie films, linking Linklater's cinephilia with that of its fans (ibid.). As academic attention to the films does not show any signs of flagging and fans wait expectantly for a fourth instalment (which, at the time of writing, is not likely to happen), their cultural status continues to grow. As a film about youth, *Before Sunrise* is closely linked to the philosophy of its predecessor *Slacker* and the 1990s white youth culture that they both came to represent. It must also be framed within the evolution of independent cinema in the 1990s, which it closely encapsulated during its production history. In this chapter we have also highlighted its contribution to the genre of romantic comedy which, rather than oppose, it rejuvenated and eventually helped to develop. The discourse of realism and the particular strategies developed by Linklater to construct it, and the narrative conventions on which it was based, were crucial in the film's, and then the trilogy's, intervention in the genre.

Additionally, the film's consideration as part of a trilogy 'in real time', in the course of which the characters grow from young adults to early middle age, also affords spectators what other films about youth cultures could not provide: a narrative of ageing beyond early adulthood and a historically grounded speculation on how youth turns into middle age – in other words, a narrative of the possible futures of youth. While this exploration has been framed within the discussion of time in many accounts of the film, not enough consideration has been given to questions relating to space: to the film's construction of romance as a matter not only of time but also of space, and the importance of Europe – of Vienna in *Before Sunrise* – as the space of the film. The realism of the temporality of the film, remarked on by the critics, is reproduced in similar strategies to construct space realistically – so much so that the film becomes not just a film about the relationship between a young man and a young woman but also a film about a transnational relationship in the explicitly transnational space of Europe constructed by the trilogy. Through this change of perspective, from national to transnational, *Before Sunrise* became part of the intensification of transnational collaborations and transnational stories in the cinema of the last three decades, a trend that at both the industrial and the cultural level has not stopped growing ever since and that together with other, more specific developments in the audio-visual industry, has dramatically changed our perception of the world and of cinematic stories. *Before Sunrise*, therefore, represents a third transition. After the transition from independent to 'indie' and from the new romances to 'walking and talking' plots, came the transition from national to transnational cinema.

As part of his exploration of the trilogy's dialogism, already mentioned above, Rob Stone describes the three films as a dialogue between American and European cinema (2018: 118). We want to point out that the dialogue does not only take place in terms of references to the history of the medium in both continents; but is, perhaps more importantly, part of the film's concern with borders and transnational culture at an important juncture in the history of Europe. Specifically, the images of youth offered by *Before Sunrise* are closely linked to the last of the list of the pleasures afforded by the film as described in the introduction to this volume: the sight of young women and men moving around Europe, which (thanks, among other things, to the success of EU initiatives like the Erasmus programme) was becoming relatively commonplace in the continent and was fostering transnational encounters, and also producing transnational problems not dissimilar to those faced by Céline and Jesse in *Before Midnight*. What is particularly remarkable is that a US independent film, with a modest amount of European funding, came to participate in this project of European integration. The film's intervention in the redefinition of the European cultural project reminds us of Harrod, Liz and Timoshkina's view that the concept of European cinema was being constructed in the interstices of the national and was to be transnational and trans-geographical from the outset (2015: 16). In the next three chapters, we will relate the formal and narrative strategies utilised by *Before Sunrise* to the film's construction of intimate protocols for a generation, as delineated above. We will also frame this particular cinematic representation of youth within the film's construction of a European space and the part played in it by, at the industrial level, a US film and, at the diegetic level, the fact that one of the protagonists is a US citizen. The resulting space is not just the environment in which the narrative of youth and romance develops but, in an important sense, also the very centre of the film, what the film and its sequels are ultimately about.

3 Falling in Love with Linklater

Genre, Realism, Quotation and Young Love

Pink Champagne

In Leo McCarey's *Love Affair* (1939), Michel Marnay (Charles Boyer), a French playboy about to marry a wealthy US heiress, finds himself travelling from Europe to New York on an ocean liner. There he meets Terry McKay (Irene Dunne), a former nightclub singer now in a relationship with a wealthy man that also happens to be her boss. They flirt, have dinner together, and try to avoid each other's company (for the sake of her reputation, mainly) but, in spite of all their efforts, end up falling in love. Before getting off the boat in New York City, they decide to break up with their respective partners and arrange to meet six months later at the top of the Empire State Building.

The film was unanimously acclaimed by contemporaneous reviewers, while it was also a box-office success. It garnered six Academy Award nominations but won none. Writing in 1946, Bob White, from the *Los Angeles Times*, speculated on the movie's disappointing results on Oscar night: 'if it hadn't been the year that David O. Selznick brought in *Gone with the Wind*, Mr. McCarey's affair would have won hands down' (1946: 23). Reviewers praised the movie's realism: 'this picture is looking at life and looking at living in its best and finest sense' (Schallert 1939: 10); the way dialogue and performance had been used to construct the growing attraction between both characters: 'half-finished phrases, a look, a silence, a whole relationship sketched sharp in a question and answer' (Lejeune 1939: 12); and the attention it paid to the detail in human interaction: 'As in all of McCarey's pictures, the greatest perfection is in the little, human scenes in which people do commonplace things or carry on commonplace talk with superb, complete naturalness; scenes in which every tiny movement or inflection is as carefully directed as a diamond cutter directs his tools' (Wales 1939: 79).

McCarey's way of working with actors never relied on a finished script. Rewrites on the day of shooting were common. Yet, as Irene Dunne claimed in an interview, whenever she was given dialogue on the set, she asked to be excused for a while to find her character's motivation for the new lines, which, in her case, were never improvised: 'As a result, the performance looks natural. But nobody realises the amount of effort you've put in' (Dunne, quoted in Viera 2013: 50–1). Julie Delpy has made similar claims in relation to the

DOI: 10.4324/9781003224334-4

improvisational look of *Before Sunrise* and the *Before* trilogy as a whole: 'They are tediously rehearsed, every detail planned, every overlapping line scripted. It's so precise that it's almost a joke when people think we are acting off the cuff' (quoted in Borrelli 2013: 5).

Leo McCarey remade his own film in 1957. The new movie, *An Affair to Remember*, starred Cary Grant in the role of the European Casanova Nicolo Ferrante and Deborah Kerr as Terry McKay. The plot of the film remained basically the same even if the film's length was increased by almost thirty minutes. It received four Academy Award nominations and, like the original film, won none. Reviews were generally positive, even if their praise fell very short of the critical enthusiasm met by *Love Affair*. Bosley Crowther, writing for the *New York Times*, for instance, describes the couple's six-months-ahead marriage pact as 'ridiculously childish for a couple of adults to make'. As Crowther rhetorically asks himself and his readers: 'Could it be, too, that a brand of make-believe that was tolerable eighteen years ago, before color and CinemaScope and other intrusions, is just a little discomforting now?' (1957). Most critics thought that the second part of the film was overlong and its pace uneven (Crowther 1957; Haynes 1957: 15).

However, as the years passed, the remake quickly dwarfed the original in popularity. Nora Ephron's 1993 *Sleepless in Seattle* immediately comes to mind. Annie Reed (Meg Ryan) knows *An Affair to Remember* by heart and, in an attempt to concoct and bring to life her own romantic fantasy, suggests the top of the Empire State as a meeting place with a widower she has fallen in love with through a radio programme. *Sleepless in Seattle* can be placed within the type of romantic comedy that Steve Neale labelled 'new romances': a trend within the genre that tries to reconcile the values of 'old-fashioned romance' with the social and cultural changes regarding sexual and intimate protocols that took place in the US from the 1960s onwards (1992: 294–9). As Neale argues, one of the ways in which this is done is by placing romantic texts from the past at the centre of the narrative. Ephron's film is not the only movie in which *An Affair to Remember* is invoked as the epitome of romance. Terry and Nicky's love story is featured and/or referenced in many other films, from *Making Love* (Hiller 1982) and *Irreconcilable Differences* (Shyer 1984) to *Au plus près du paradis* (Marshall 2002) and *Touch of Pink* (Rashid 2004), to name just a few. References to *Love Affair*, on the contrary, are scarce (according to the Internet Movie Database it is only featured in the 2000 film *Happy Accidents* [Anderson]).

An Affair to Remember, therefore, has gained a place in the cultural imagination to represent old-fashioned romance, while *Love Affair* has receded into relative oblivion. Both, however, immediately come to mind when watching *Before Sunrise* and the lovers' impromptu decision to meet six months later. When Jesse and Céline – a couple formed, like in the other two films, by a European and an American – are about to part ways forever at the station, Jesse tells her that he does not want to stick to their previous decision that theirs was going to be just a one-off encounter. Céline confesses that she was waiting for him to say it and suggests that maybe they should meet again in five years' time. As Céline's train is about to leave, five years hurriedly become six months. Pressed for time, Jesse's six-months-ahead date is presented as an off-the-top-of-his-head suggestion, as is shown by the way he shrugs his shoulders and briskly tilts his head to the left when suggesting the new date. Céline and Jesse share with the new romances of the 1990s the way in which they approach romantic love with both ardent belief and cynical distance but, unlike Annie Reed and other fictional characters who are movie-savvy enough to pass off some specific behaviour as an imitation of a popular culture text, Jesse's suggestion does not feel like a self-conscious reference to a classical movie. Yet, the connection is impossible to miss for those familiar with one or both of McCarey's movies, especially because this is a film in which cinematic references abound, as has been abundantly discussed by, among others, Robin Wood (1998: 318–35), James MacDowell (2008), Rob Stone (2018: 116–20) and Murray Smith (2021a: 83–101). The connections with McCarey's films become even more evident in *Before Sunset*, when we find out that, like in the earlier films, the male character made it to the appointment but the female character did not for reasons beyond her control. Likewise, in all three films, the couple's belated reunion, which takes place right before the male character is about to embark on a transatlantic journey, is made possible by an artistic creation on the part of the male character: a painting in the case of Marnay and Ferrante and a novel in the case of Jesse.

The parallels, therefore, are striking, but as soon as we notice them, the differences come to the fore: for instance, unlike Jesse's, Marnay's and Ferrante's six-month temporal window is a rather meditated one. Both loafers, who have been living off their charms for most of their adult lives, need time to find a proper way of earning a living before marrying Terry. In this sense, the two McCarey movies do not only abide by the convention of 'marriage for the wrong reason vs marriage for the right reason' (a constant in romantic comedies from, at least the screwball tradition that is contemporaneous to *Love Affair*), they also seem to imply that Marnay and Ferrante need to put their masculinity to a socially sanctioned use: anything but becoming 'one of those useless, good-for-nothing gigolos', as Lily (Miriam Hopkins) eloquently puts it in Lubitsch's *Trouble in Paradise* (1932). Jesse and Céline's plans for their future meeting, on the contrary, do not go beyond the desire to see each other again and 'keep talking', which is precisely the reason Jesse invokes when he asks Céline to get off the train with him in the first place. If *Before Sunrise* were using its many cinematic sources in a more self-conscious manner, it could be easily argued that the characters want to keep on drinking 'pink champagne': McCarey's films' metonymic way of referring to sex and sexual desire.

In the referential game, the parallels and differences are of equal importance: the similarities draw the audience's attention to the cinematic and cultural past and provide a prestigious context and a specific point of reference for the new film and then the differences guarantee historical plausibility to its new cultural meanings. Wales's adulatory description of *Love Affair*, quoted above, uncannily reads as an accurate account of *Before Sunrise* and of Linklater's much-vaunted branch of realism across the decades. Equally striking are Dunne's and Delpy's very similar comments about their experiences with their respective films. They show that the vocabulary to describe cultural verisimilitude and professional commitment to performance has remained relatively constant. But this common ground makes the discrepancies more visible. For our purposes in this book, age immediately comes to the fore: the age of the protagonists of the first two films, on the one hand, and of those of the 'new' film, on the other. We know that Céline and Jesse are in their early twenties. There are no explicit references to the ages of the protagonists of McCarey's two films. We know that Irene Dunne was forty-one when *Love Affair* was released and Charles Boyer, forty. Cary Grant was fifty-three and Deborah Kerr thirty-six in *An Affair to Remember*. Beyond the age difference between the man and the woman in the latter (a far from unusual occurrence in the Hollywood films of the 1950s), the four McCarey characters are clearly much older, and in different age brackets, than youthful Jesse and Céline. *Before Sunrise* is interested in a very different type of experience of falling in love from the other two. *Love Affair* and *An Affair to Remember* are about mature men and women falling in love. Linklater's film is about the experience of youthful love. Keeping in mind the two earlier 'affairs', we will focus on Céline and Jesse's youth and the key role it plays in portraying the emotional connection between them. Drawing on the cultural context described in Chapter 1, we will frame this discussion in historical terms. But before we do that, we first concentrate on the most obvious narrative difference between *Before Sunrise* and its predecessors; namely, the fact that in McCarey's two films the promise to meet six months later takes place halfway through the movie while *Before Sunrise* turns it into one of the film's most famous features: its open ending.

'Later'

For a movie with such obvious generic connections at its very heart, academic and critical consensus about the film's realism may seem surprising, ironic even. The same could be argued about the director's well-known penchant for over-rehearsing in order to achieve a naturalistic performance and about the apparently random narrative structure of the film which is, in fact, rather contrived, as has been eloquently argued by Wood (1998) and Norton (2000), among others. Yet, this does not invalidate the film's well-known 'realist' credentials. As Aaron Cutler suggests, films flaunting a 'naturalistic register' do not always have a bigger claim at representing reality than those that are overly 'stagy or false'. In fact, for Cutler, films can best capture 'reality not by reproducing the truth of daily life, but rather through registering how peo-ple create fictions throughout it' (2013: 28). As suggested in Chapter 2, the 'realism' of *Before Sunrise* is steeped in generic, performative and narrative conventions. Céline and Jesse's encounter on the train and the time they spend together in Vienna is not 'the truth of daily life' but rather a romantic fantasy of immediate connection with a stranger that is not so different from conven-tional romcom fare such as *Love Affair* and *An Affair to Remember*. Yet, while these two have a second part in which we witness some of the obstacles that hinder the final reunion of the couple, *Before Sunrise* leaves the characters' six-months-ahead reunion in a cinematic limbo.

The open ending of *Before Sunrise* can be approached through Richard Neupert's category of Open Story films, that is, those movies in which the narrative discourse is finished but the story is left unresolved or incomplete (Neupert 1995: 32–3). At the level of discourse (or syuzhet), *Before Sunrise* is a Closed Text. It is carefully bracketed by, at the beginning, the opening shots of the railroads and the landscapes seen from a moving train and, at the end, the shots of the empty streets of Vienna and the final shots of Jesse and Céline before the fade-to-black. The soundtrack is also carefully designed and two pieces of classical music, the French overture of Purcell's *Dido and Aeneas* and the *Andante* movement of Bach's *Sonata for Viola da Gamba and Harpsichord* BWV 1027 are heard over the opening and the closing shots, respectively. There are even two mirroring shots of a woman dressed in brown in a similar train compartment at the beginning and at the end of the film (the first, an extra, the second, Céline). At the level of the story (or fabula), though, Jesse and Céline's last-minute decision to change their minds about their only night together suddenly leaves the story wide open. In typical romantic com-edy fashion, the characters change their mind at the very last minute about their imminent, for-good, separation. They kiss again, make a pact to reunite in six months and part ways.

For Neupert, Open Story films often 'motivate and justify their failure to resolve by appealing to a realistic aesthetic' (1995: 75). Neupert's choice of words is not random here: the movies he is discussing *fail* to resolve because the problems at stake, he claims, are usually unresolvable. Defenders of this type of movies, Neupert argues, usually read a movie's lack of closure as a rejection of artificial storytelling norms and an attempt to represent the con-tingency and ambiguity of real life (76). The open ending of *Before Sunrise*, on the other hand, is not a failure to resolve but rather a deliberately ambigu-ous stopping point. It could be argued that any movie needs to stop at some point and that, as MacDowell has argued, one of the most emblematic movie endings, the reunion of a happy couple, is always more a beginning than an ending (MacDowell 2013: passim). In this sense, Neupert's definition of Open Story films as those that suspend the story 'before all diegetic events are finished' (1995: 75) is problematic *per se*. Most movie endings only aim at re-establishing the order that was disrupted at the beginning, but it is clear that life goes on and diegetic events are not finished. Or, as Robert Altman used to say whenever he was asked about his penchant for open endings: 'death is the only ending I know' (quoted in Keogh 2000: 160). Yet, what is different about the ending of *Before Sunrise* is that the couple's arrangement to meet six months later is not just a more or less convenient stopping point but one that deliberately poses a question only to leave it unanswered. As Robin Wood puts it: 'everyone with whom I have watched it immediately raises the question of whether or not Jesse and Céline will keep their six-months-ahead date' (1998: 163). In the cinematic context of the twenty-first century in which movie franchises and sequels are the order of the day, this type of ending would probably be routinely read as a cliffhanger that leaves one narrative thread unresolved to open the way for a sequel. However, in 1995, when *Before Sunrise* was released, the sequel was in nobody's mind and when it happened, nine years later, it did not start where the previous film had left it.

MacDowell has argued that *Before Sunrise* stands somewhere in between Neupert's categories of Open Story films and Closed Text films (those in which both the discourse and the story are closed by the movie's end). He relates this state of in-betweenness to Anthony Giddens's notion of romance as introducing 'a narrative in a person's life' (1992: 39). For MacDowell, as long as Jesse and Céline's time in Vienna was just a one-off encounter and, therefore, a celebration of a moment, theirs was an Open Story. Yet, the fact that Jesse and Céline fall in love 'recasts the characters of what easily could be a goal-less, Open Story "Art film" as, effectively, protagonists in an "unfinished" Closed Text romance narrative' (2021b: 179). It is clear from the above quotation that MacDowell is recasting the definition of Open Story texts by adding conventions that are not related to a movie's ending. The fact that Open Story movies have tended to feature characters without clear goals (as is the case, for example, of Altman's movies) does not mean that lack of goals must be a feature of that type of movie. Besides, Jesse makes his goal very clear to Céline fifteen minutes into the film: 'I want to keep talking to you'. This is Jesse's goal at the beginning of the film and it is, without a doubt, one he attains with flying colours.

Carlo Cenciarelli has explored the role and meanings of the *Andante* from Bach's sonata from the moment in which Jesse starts walking away from Céline's train to the film's final fade-to-black. As he puts it, during the *temps mort* sequence of the city at dawn 'Vienna is emptied of the characters' on-screen presence but filled with music that sustains the significance of their encounter' (2018: 176). It is easy to agree with Cenciarelli's interpretation of the musical piece over the shots of the empty Vienna, which he compares and contrasts with the diegetic harpsichord piece heard before. Cenciarelli highlights the sense of flow evoked by Bach's *Andante*, which literally means something that is moving or walking. After sunrise, life goes on and the city is impervious to the million stories, desires and anxieties traversing its streets (a direct link to Céline's observation in church when she marvels at the ability of places to 'hold the pain and happiness of so many generations') [see Figures 3.1–3.2].

Figures 3.1–3.2 Vienna after Céline and Jesse

Hans Maes has related these empty shots of Vienna, which he refers to as the 'Ozu sequence', to the general feeling of melancholy – understood as the bitter-sweet emotional process triggered by a realisation about a fact of human existence that puts our whole life in context – that he finds in *Before Sunrise* (and also in the *Before* trilogy as a whole) (2021: 41–64).

In this sense, one of the most meaningful shots, because of the traces the two protagonists have carelessly left there, is that of the park at dawn in the *temps mort* sequence. The signifiers of the culmination of Céline and Jesse's memorable night, an empty bottle of wine and two glasses, are now just trash lying on the grass [see Figure 3.3]. Like the garbage being collected in Venice at the beginning of *Trouble in Paradise*, the signifiers of romantic love look different once the lovers are gone and the spell is broken. An old

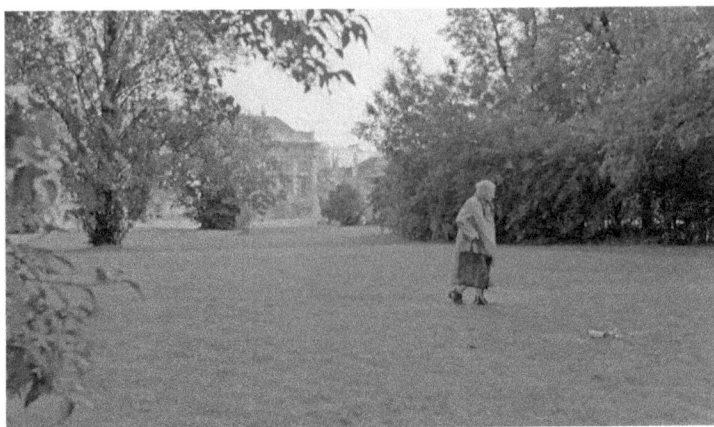

Figure 3.3 Love the morning after

lady, dressed in brown and limping slowly, passes by and exits the shot frame right. Given the emphasis that the film has put on old age, the presence of this unnamed character does not go unnoticed. The character especially resonates with Céline's feelings of being an old woman on her deathbed reminiscing about her youth but also with her grandmother's story about her lifelong love (not her husband) and with Jesse's story about seeing his great-grandmother's ghost. It also reminds us that the unnamed character was also young once and, therefore, she becomes a visual reminder of the Latin trope '*collige, virgo, rosas*', an invitation to the young characters to enjoy the vitality and beauty of youth while it lasts. It also resonates with an earlier shot in this sequence, which also includes an unnamed elderly character, this time a man with a bag in his hand walking left until he disappears behind the Moses Fountain in the middle of Franziskaner Platz – the place where Jesse joked about the monks not wearing any underwear and laughed at the palm-reader [see Figure 3.4]. The shot between these two is that of the now empty bank of the Danube. In the background, two trains going in opposite directions cross paths for an instant and then go their separate ways, literally mirroring Jesse and Céline's brief crossing of paths in *Before Sunrise*.

Most illuminating in Cenciarelli's analysis of the film's ending is his observation about how the movie's particular rendition of the sonata's *Andante* is made to stop in a half cadence, 'just before the final chord'. A half cadence gives an unresolved feeling to a phrase. It creates tension because it is unfinished. For Cenciarelli, this half cadence suggests the refusal to embrace a predetermined trajectory and remains suspended in an indeterminate state full of possibilities (2018: 177). In this sense, the piece, also unfinished, mirrors the big question posed by the movie's ending. The answer to the question came with the release of *Before Sunset*. Yet, for nine years, Céline and Jesse

Figure 3.4 Old man with a bag at the Moses Fountain

were caught in a suspended state similar to that of the Schrödinger's cat paradox (both alive and dead until the box has been opened and the state of the cat has been observed), having both reunited and not reunited at the same time. This idea of 'infinite potential' has close links with the parallel reality scenario voiced out by the talkative taxi passenger played by Linklater at the beginning of *Slacker* and, therefore, was not very far removed from the director's concerns at the time. The sense of full possibilities of the open ending is also related to Linklater's particular view of the slacker ethos (discussed in Chapter 1) and to the age of the characters: two emerging adults traversing 'the age of possibilities' (Arnett 2005).

'Let's Just Be Rational Adults About This'

After Céline and Jesse have shaken hands on their one-night-only pact, they go to a nightclub to get a bottle of wine. While Céline steals a couple of glasses, Jesse persuades the barman to give him a bottle for free (or on the vague promise that he will pay for it once he is back in the US). 'For the greatest night of your life', says the amiable barman as he gives the bottle to Jesse. Lou Christie's 1965 song 'Trapeze', about the ups and downs of romantic love, is playing on the soundtrack. As Jesse leaves the frame to reunite with Céline, the camera stays with the barman, who stares at the young couple with a look that suggests both his nostalgia for the vitality and determination of young love and his awareness of the fact that, like in Christie's song, 'love is like a trapeze' and disappointment is often around the corner [see Figure 3.5]. This moment may be the closest we come to the 'pink champagne' scene in the early part of *Love Affair* and *An Affair to Remember*, a scene in which

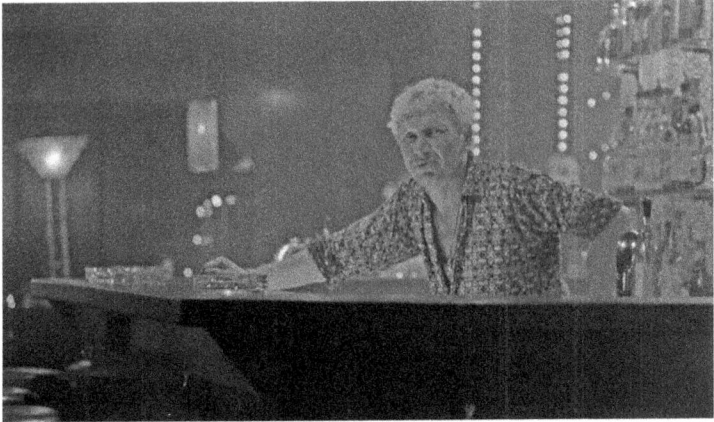

Figure 3.5 In awe of the vitality of youth

audiences probably do not even remember the unnamed character behind the bar. In McCarey's films, the pink champagne stands as a close metonymy of the growing desire and sexual affinity that spectators, as much as the characters, perceive between Terry and Michel/Nicolo, even as they struggle to hide it from everyone around them. Céline and Jesse, for whom the obstacles, such as they are at this moment, come exclusively from within the couple, see their impending sexual union openly celebrated by the barman. He is one of several anonymous characters Jesse and Céline meet during their time together. These apparently random encounters are part of the overall episodic structure of the movie, which still bears traces of the narrative pattern of the director's first movie, *Slacker*. Through each of these encounters, Céline and Jesse learn something about the other and, in the process, start falling in love.

In a review written right after the film's release, Michael Wilmington claims that watching *Before Sunrise* is like falling in love (1995). Wilmington's enthusiastic review highlights the process through which, while the characters are falling in love with each other, spectators are falling in love with the fantasy of their encounter, with the dream of cultural seduction, with the city of Vienna and with the beguiling references to classical and European movie romance. As he puts it, 'there is a heightened, nervous awareness about *Before Sunrise* that has a swimmingly uneasy effect. It opens up vulnerable veins and ducts' (1995: C). Even if most reviewers shared Wilmington's appreciation for the film, not everybody was so impressed by the relationship between its two young characters. Some refused to see it as anything other than an expression of Gen X apathy. Amy Gamerman, writing for *The Wall Street Journal*, claimed

> *Before Sunrise* is not the most boring movie around, perhaps because its two stars seem very real as the disaffected, inquisitive kids they play [...]

But after watching Delpy and Hawke get their fortunes told, play pinball and schmooze in various cafes and clubs, I grew itchy for adult company (quoted in '*Sunrise* over Criticism' 1995: 52).

For Manohla Dargis, the film is mainly about two twentysomethings indifferently 'swapping theories and banalities about sex, love and death' (1995: 33). What seems to emerge from the few negative reviews is a reluctance to see beyond the connotations behind the Gen X stereotype (of the director, the male lead and the fictional characters) and engage with the hesitations, insecurities and contradictions of the film's particular portrayal of young love. Significantly, Dargis would change her tune in her enthusiastic review of *Before Sunset*, in which, for the critic, the fact that the characters are older and 'the years have beautifully mellowed the actors and their director' makes the couple's second meeting in Paris 'a deeper and truer work of art' (2004).

Psychologists Margaret S. Clark and Lindsey A. Beck have described the initiation of relationships among emerging adults as a 'complicated and skilled' dance that needs to sync three independent but interrelated processes: strategic self-presentation, evaluation of the potential partner and self-protection from rejection (2011: 193–5). The processes, they argue, are not exclusive to this life stage but become central to it because of other concomitant processes characteristic of the stage such as the process of identity exploration, the instability regarding sexual partners and, especially, the sense that emerging adulthood is the age of possibilities, a life stage in which, as Arnett has argued, almost everything seems possible and individuals have more options to choose from than they ever had or will have in the future (2004: 16–7). Delpy's and Hawke's nuanced and carefully orchestrated performances in *Before Sunrise* convey Clark and Beck's three processes simultaneously. After their casual encounter on the train, we see them strategically presenting their best self to each other while choosing conversation topics and being aware of the fact that they are being looked at and listened to. Both characters marvel at the emotional and intellectual connection they are feeling with the other and carefully measure each step to avoid the feeling of rejection that could come with a rushed move. Detailed analyses of some of the movie's best-known scenes, such as the listening booth long take or the fake phone conversation game at the café, have highlighted how performance and film style combine to put forward the characters' burgeoning desire for each other using a realist aesthetic (see, for instance, Wood 1998 and Norton 2000). Yet, together with that nascent desire, what the film also shows is the characters acting and voicing out a series of cultural scripts that, while not hampering their desire for each other, have an impact on the way in which this desire is formulated, acted out and also constrained.

Following some of the findings in Ann Swidler's sociological study *Talk of Love* (2001), MacDowell has analysed Jesse and Céline's oscillation between two sets of attitudes to love and relationships in *Before Sunrise*: the prosaic-realist view of love that sustains that romantic attraction dwindles over time and, as a result, makes love relationships by definition short-lived, and the mythic view of love that includes the forever and the one-and-only qualities of what Giddens (1992) refers to as the 'romantic love complex' (2013: 142–5). At the beginning of their encounter, Jesse's and Céline's strategic presentations of themselves clearly endorse the prosaic-realist view of love. In the scene at the fair, for instance, we find them, in typical Gen X fashion, showing their disdain for the cultural scripts of romantic love. Both seem to agree on the fact that romantic relationships are not built to last: Jesse's parents ended up divorcing and, in his opinion, should have done it sooner; Céline's parents are together and apparently happy, but her grandmother's confession that she had spent her whole life in love with a man not her husband casts a doubt on the possibility of genuine romantic relationships. While Céline is concerned with the fact that one could live his/her own whole life as a lie, Jesse thinks that it was better that her grandmother never married the man she was in love with, because the fulfilment of any romantic fantasy inevitably leads to disappointment. Not very convinced by Jesse's cynical view of romantic love (which she sees as a pose), Céline mocks his previous behaviour on the Ferris wheel, when he unabashedly invoked well-known romantic clichés to ask her to kiss him. These instances show that, like characters in the new romances, the two young protagonists of the film deftly navigate the two discourses in order to have their (romantic) cake and eat it, too. Later conversations start to show clear dents in their apparently watertight prosaic-realistic façades. Jesse, who describes love as 'an escape for two people that don't know how to be alone', seems fascinated by the silent (and, even if he does not say, very romantic) protocols of a Quaker wedding he once attended, and Céline confesses that she has trouble combining her desire for independence with the fact that 'loving and being loved' mean a lot to her.

The clash between the two attitudes peaks in the scene in which the characters make their 'one-night-only pact'. On the café-restaurant boat, one of Jesse's stories about the finiteness of existence leads Céline to remark that this is probably their only night together. She had previously mentioned it to her imaginary friend on the fake phone conversation, but the issue had not been discussed yet between them. Jesse seems genuinely shocked at the thought and rephrases Céline's point as a question, which she immediately bounces back at him. As he starts to articulate a hesitant answer, she cuts him short and points out that they live on two different continents. Before the possibility (and impracticalities) of a transcontinental relationship are even laid on the table, Céline asks Jesse to be rational adults about it and suggests a different approach.

Apparently, the prosaic-realistic view of love takes centre stage in Céline's proposal. Both seem to be aware of the fact that the romantic convention 'love conquers all' is a lie and know that their growing desire for each other will inevitably fade away once their Viennese slacking diversion is over. Aware and afraid of the obvious difficulties ahead if they decide to meet again, they prefer to celebrate their hours left together and, in order to protect their emotional connection, cut it short in full bloom, which will freeze it in a sort of eternal present – their own 'magical moment', according to Céline's definition of magic in an earlier scene. Both characters try to argue against the idea that a relationship that does not last forever is a failed one, in a way similar to that of the 'pure relationship' theorised by Giddens (1992). Yet, unlike in the pure relationship, they are not even going to let the relationship run its course, which also implies a separation from the prosaic-realistic view of love. Oddly enough, by taking the idea of romance (understood in Giddens's sense of story or trajectory) out of their relationship, the young lovers seem to be after the immutability of the romantic love complex, that type of love that, in Shakespeare's words, does not alter 'when it alteration finds'.

Not surprisingly, neither Jesse nor Céline seem too convinced about the pact they are about to make, which, like their attempts to repress the feelings they are afraid to share with each other at this moment, is bursting at the seams. Slightly shocked by Céline's pessimism and reluctant to believe what she has just said, Jesse asks her the question twice: 'But you think tonight is it, huh? I mean, that tonight is our only night?' 'It's the only way, no?', replies Céline, desperately hoping to get a 'no' for an answer. The moment they commit to the plan, Johann Strauss the Younger's 'Wiener Blut' waltz starts playing on the soundtrack and Jesse points at the two musicians serenading four customers sitting at a table near them, the shot of the musicians providing some relief from the suffocating shot/reverse-shot conversation. The piece was written to celebrate the royal wedding of Archduchess Gisela Louise Maria and Prince Leopold of Bavaria, which took place in Vienna in 1873. Its lively rhythm and its romantic love connotations clash with the characters' decision to put a rein to their desire to meet again after that night. Even if Jesse tries to ease the poignancy of the moment with the handshake that seals their pact and their premature farewells, Céline's eyes, filling up with tears, tell a different story [see Figure 3.6]. A second later, she turns around to look at the musicians off-screen, as if she was trying to find some consolation (and distance) in the romantic music of the past. In *Love Affair* or *An Affair to Remember*, 'Wiener Blut' would have probably been framed very differently, not with the detachment that makes the lovers notice it but at the same time allows them to keep their distance from its romantic connotations. In a sense, the earlier lovers' maturity leads them to acknowledge the irrationality of their affair, to foresee the bumpy road ahead, but still see it through to the end, afraid of the future but not allowing potential disappointment to repress their desire.

The realism found by Wales in *Love Affair* is, as we have seen, the main component of the critical success of *Before Sunrise* and of the trilogy, and a central ingredient of its fan base. Yet, both formally and culturally, it is a very different type of realism. Both films excel at portraying the humanity of the characters, but this is a humanity that exists in a very different age and at a very different period of life. At this climactic moment, Jesse and Céline

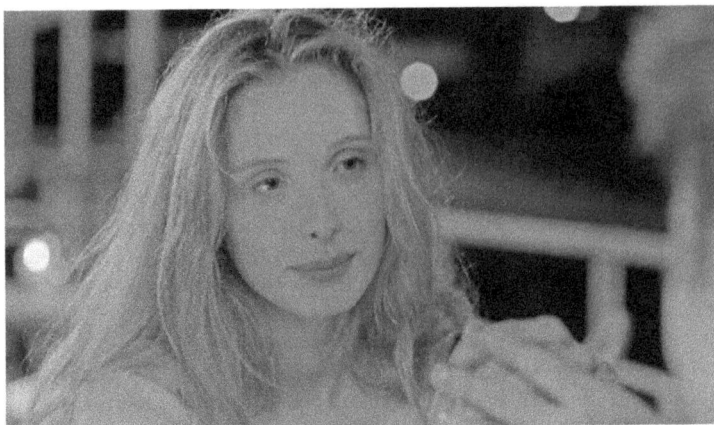

Figure 3.6 Céline is upset at their decision to rein in desire

are being human in the immature romanticism of their decision. One of the problems with their vow (and the reason why they cannot keep it at the end of the film) is that Céline's proposal was framed as both adult and rational. Romantic love has traditionally been described as irrational. Its prosaic-realist version is usually considered a more rational approach. Yet, the young lovers' pact is not rational. In fact, as argued above, in their desire for immutability, their pact becomes highly romantic and, in turn, irrational. Besides, Céline and Jesse are not adults yet. They are emerging adults, a distinctive and different life stage from adulthood, and, therefore, are using the wrong lens to consider their options, which is forcing them to drastically narrow down the options ahead. The prosaic view of love is one more attuned to adult love and commitments. They seem to have forgotten that, as (white, middle-class) emerging adults and slackers, they are travellers of the age of possibilities. The slacking ethos that got them off the train together in Vienna cannot be repressed all of a sudden to keep their youthful desire preserved in amber. As Céline put it earlier on in their conversation in the alley, risks must be taken, because 'the answer must be in the attempt'. In this sense, the answer to the question haunting the film's open ending becomes irrelevant, since it is the attempt, and not the outcome, that matters. It is precisely the film's staunch belief in the attempt that places this movie within a very specific comic tradition, as will be argued in Chapter 6.

4 Crossing the Ocean

From Regional to Transnational

The Journey to the Border

As we argued in Chapter 2, the move from San Antonio to Vienna and from the US to Europe would prove crucial not only in the final form of the film but in the place that it came to occupy in the history of cinema. Independent (or, subsequently, 'indie') US films of the 1990s often set stories about young people and their relationships in recognisable, local surroundings. The plots of movies like *Singles*, *Ruby in Paradise* (Núñez 1993), *The Brothers McMullen*, *Beautiful Girls*, *Walking and Talking*, *The Truth about Cats and Dogs* (Lehman 1996) and *Romy and Michele's High School Reunion* (Mirkin 1997), among others, take place in US cities and suburbs; the young people's interests, hopes and anxieties are mostly circumscribed to their immediate surroundings – whether their childhood homes or the places where they live – and the characters' mobility potential tends to be modest. This outlook affects their cultural identity as much as their romantic protocols. Transnational concerns are beyond the films' remits and the characters' interests. The geographical specificity of *Slacker* and *Dazed and Confused* and Linklater's links with Austin, situated his early career in a similar context, one which Rob Stone relates to regional cinema, a notion that to him encapsulated much of what had been distinctive about US independent cinema since the 1970s (2013: 9–10). Beyond Linklater's and Krizan's imprint, *Before Sunrise* originated as a project within this independent imagination. Yet, the move to Vienna triggered a new set of concerns, similar to those that would become more widespread only a few years later in the cinema of the new century and, specifically, in cinematic representations of youth cultures and relationships. Thus, *Before Sunrise* became a direct precedent of the turn to transnational culture in twenty-first century cinema.

It is not only that the film takes place in Vienna and that its female protagonist is a young French woman travelling between two European countries and then spending a few hours with a young man from the US in a third European country. The fact that the basic scenario was initially conceived as involving an American couple in an American city meant that Linklater and Krizan, with the later contribution of Delpy and Hawke, were forced to undertake a process of adaptation of their story and characters to a European space and a

DOI: 10.4324/9781003224334-5

transnational relationship. Thus, the journey from local to transnational was part of the writing process and is stamped in the film: in the way the characters relate to each other, in the way they gradually become attracted to and fall in love with each other, and, crucially for a 'walking and talking' film, in the dynamic and content of their dialogues. Neither falling into clichés nor altogether rejecting them, Céline and Jesse's protracted conversations undergo a reflexive transformation that takes them from a national to a transnational context. In spite of historical ups and downs, actions and reactions in the last twenty-five years or so, this transnational conversation has since become widespread in films, and familiar to spectators, both in Europe and around the world.

As the two young characters grew older and reappeared on the screens twice at nine years' intervals, the shape of the industry around them changed and similar stories of transnational relationships between young people proliferated. If we take as a sample four films from the two following decades that were openly indebted to *Before Sunrise*, the evolution from local to transnational becomes more apparent. *In Search of a Midnight Kiss* (2007) and *500 Days of Summer* (2009) both feature twenty-something American couples meeting and talking, and falling in and out of love in Los Angeles. *Monsters* (2010) is about two young US citizens meeting in extreme circumstances in Central America and falling in love as they walk through the Northern Mexican borderlands. *Already Tomorrow in Hong Kong* (2015), the closest to Linklater's film, tells the story of the encounter of an Asian American woman from California and a Jewish American man from New York who meet, walk and talk in Hong Kong. By the time Emily Ting's little-seen movie came out, Jesse and Céline had already prolonged their relationship for eighteen years and two more films, and had continued their walks, conversations and, eventually, fights in Paris and the southern Peloponnese. Borders, which seemed mostly far away from the stories' locations in the independent films of the 1990s, increasingly became not only present but part of the films' narrative and formal construction and of their thematic concerns in the following two decades. Not only did more films tell border-crossing stories but borders and borderlands became more pervasive, whether at the actual boundaries between countries or far away from them, in cinematic narratives.

The Cosmopolitan Lens 1: Theory

The rise of transnational cinema, of which *Before Sunrise* became an early example within the corpus of 1990s films about youth, has brought about a change in critical paradigms in Film Studies, as witness for instance the appearance of the academic journal *Transnational Cinemas* (later *Transnational Screens*) in 2010. Although the relation between national and transnational has been the subject of much debate (Shaw 2013: 48–51), in historical terms at least, the expansion of the transnational is closely linked to the crisis of the national. At the beginning of the twenty-first century, Ulrich Beck and Nathan Sznaider called for a change of perspective in the field of sociology: from a methodological nationalism, in which the nation was at the centre of social research, to a methodological cosmopolitanism that accounted for the fact that, in a global world, nations had lost some of their relevance (2006: 1). They were not asking for a substitution of the cosmopolitan for the national but, rather, for a different methodology of analysis: one that used the growing body of cosmopolitan theory to construct a new way of looking at social relationships and social phenomena beyond the nation. This book shares this way of looking – this cosmopolitan lens – to explore the important dynamics brought about by the irruption of transnational culture in the process of creation of *Before Sunrise*.

A national perspective or a national methodology in historical and cultural analysis had become dominant since, at least, the end of World War I and the end of the European empires and their splintering into nations (Appiah 2018: 77; Norwich 2006: 859). Does the deployment of a cosmopolitan perspective mean that we now live in a cosmopolitan age? As we will see, that depends on the way in which we choose to define cosmopolitanism. For Robert Fine, the social forces that have ushered changes in the paradigm are an economic globalisation characterised by the free flow of capital and commerce, the intensification of movement and mixing of people, and the increase of global risks. For Fine, the age of cosmopolitanism, is, like Kant's Age of Enlightenment, more a project, a social imaginary, than a 'cosmopolitan reality'; more a philosophical perspective for viewing the potentialities of our age than an objective characterisation of the age itself (2006: 246–7). The use of the cosmopolitan lens will, therefore, also bring to the surface moments, attitudes and relationships that are not so cosmopolitan – in films as much as in the real world.

What is cosmopolitanism? The answer is more elusive than it may seem at first sight. It is, to a great extent, the degree of complexity achieved by the concept in theoretical formulations, including the acknowledgement of contradictions and dark areas, that makes the concept particularly useful. Fozdar and Woodward argue that it is a subject position, one that implies a moral obligation (2021: 4). This subject position – this way of being in the world – includes the defence of human rights (Fine 2009: 20), the practice of solidarity (Fine 2012: 379–81), world citizenry, human dignity and diversity (Skrbiš and Woodward 2013: 40, 43), the celebration of difference within universal equality (Appiah 1997: 635), and the pursuit of what Gerard Delanty calls 'the cosmopolitan moment', a moment of openness to others and the reflexive transformation that such an openness brings about (2006: 27). For Delanty, cosmopolitanism is a normative idea about the value of taking into account the other's point of view and placing oneself into a wider whole – the 'cosmos' (2014: 2).

Yet, for all its lofty aspirations, the ethical and political ambiguity of cosmopolitanism has not gone unnoticed. Jackie Stacey, for example, critiques the easy optimism of a cosmopolitanism that places prejudice and aversion elsewhere, in the other rather than in ourselves (2017: 171). Often cosmopolitan attitudes have turned into the type of celebration of diversity that originates from and can only be shared by first world citizens. Walter Mignolo mistrusts dominant descriptions of cosmopolitanism as a new version of the colonial and imperial projects. As an antidote, he proposes 'border thinking', which for him means looking from the other side of the border and adopting the subaltern's perspective (2011: 330–31). Others argue that cosmopolitanism does not necessarily involve ethical thinking. For Skrbiš and Woodward, what at first sight might appear to be genuine attitudes and ethical positionings are often a social performance, 'a flexible, available set of cultural practices and outlooks which are mobilised depending on social and cultural contexts' (2013: 129). There is a specific cosmopolitan competency that allows 'cosmopolitan' individuals to manage social difference in ways that may reproduce patterns of cultural power. In sum, rather than behave according to a cosmopolitan ethical code, some people perform cosmopolitanism for their own gain or simply for social prestige. Eurocentrism and neocolonialism are accusations that have often been cast on the concept, i.e., the claim that Europe or the West is superior as a civilisation to the rest of the world. Delanty himself acknowledges the 'latent Eurocentrism' that is present in cosmopolitan theory, even though, as some critics, including Mignolo, would argue, contemporary cosmopolitanism is precisely the production of non-Eurocentric interpretations of the world (2014: 2, 5). Put succinctly, and more generally, as Craig Calhoun argues, the problem with cosmopolitanism is that it 'is not free-floating, not equally available to everyone, not equally empowering for everyone' (2008: 434).

What we may call the dark side, or the dark history, of cosmopolitanism is, consequently, a necessary antidote to the excess of optimism that insufficiently nuanced celebrations of its egalitarian aspirations may run the risk of falling into. At the same time, charges of Eurocentrism may too readily collapse the wide geographical, political and social variety as well as the long history of the continent within a single, undifferentiated whole (which also includes the US and other 'western' countries): not everything that has happened in Europe in the course of history is or has been 'Eurocentric'. As Delanty puts it, Eurocentrism as a critical concept suffers from a one-sided view of the European heritage that overstates colonialism in the making of Europe (2014: 9).

As can be seen, ethical, normative *and* critical approaches to the concept remain, to a great extent, theoretical and largely overlook what we might call cosmopolitan realities. Alexa Robertson argues that globalisation is making people cosmopolitan 'by default' (2012: 178). The implication is that we all, to a greater or lesser extent, experience the realities of cosmopolitanism – not necessarily in a normative or a critical way, not, in many cases, concerned by its moral dimensions. Sometimes cosmopolitan experiences are born out of necessity. This is the case of the 'abject cosmopolitans' explored by Peter Nyers: those global migrants who exist on the margins of globalisation, are deprived of basic human rights, and experience cosmopolitanism in their attempts to resist their marginalisation (2003: 1073–5). Ian Woodward and Nina Høy-Petersen call our attention to the everyday contradictions of cosmopolitan subjects: in an environment in which the elitist and the fashionable meet with the utopian and the radically egalitarian, people must balance multiple conflicting cosmopolitan and parochial ethical and self-interested practices (2018: 664). For them, a cosmopolitan subject, rather than somebody living according to certain cosmopolitan principles, is somebody making everyday decisions in a cosmopolitan environment. In this context, cosmopolitanism may be, as Felicia Chan suggests, about learning to live with paradoxes and testing the limits of one's tolerance and ethical choices (2017: 141–2). Høy-Petersen and Woodward affirm that cosmopolitanism is a 'messy, conflicting and often unpredictable' set of processes and attitudes towards the increased mobility of people and things (2018: 656).

This every day, messy cosmopolitanism seems at odds with the cosmopolitan ideals outlined above and questions the sweeping generalisations of some ideological indictments, but is often closer to the realities of people living in a global, highly connected world. Utopian views of a future of borderless movements of people, universal rights, peaceful coexistence and world citizenship often clash with renewed exclusionary nationalism, securitised borders, abuses of human rights and expanding inequalities (Fozdar and Woodward 2021: 6), as well as with our personal and interpersonal difficulties to behave in consistent ways towards those that are different from us.

For our purposes, this messy variety of cosmopolitanism is often visible in the cinema's fictional narratives, which often revolve around conflicts that originate in transnational and transcultural contexts. In this sense, a cosmopolitan perspective that aspires to describe a world and a cinema of transnational exchanges within a globalised economic logic must incorporate contradiction and ambivalence and even accommodate anti-cosmopolitan attitudes. Such a subject position for the study of films must, therefore, be equally ethical, critical and descriptive, explicative rather than normative. This complex, often contradictory position, constitutes the cosmopolitan vantage point from which *Before Sunrise* is explored in this and the following chapter.

Finally, although such a cosmopolitan lens can be potentially used to analyse any contemporary film because of their existence in a global, increasingly transnational context, some films are more explicitly transnational than others in the centrality that borders take in their narratives as well as in their production. The borderliness of transnational cinema is shared with much cosmopolitan theory, which often situates borders, borderspaces and borderlands at the centre of the cosmopolitan imagination (Beck and Sznaider 2006: 1; Rovisco 2013: 150; Cooper and Rumford 2011: 262). Mignolo describes his response to Eurocentric cosmopolitanism as 'border thinking' (2011: 330) and Cooper and Rumford define 'borderwork' as the activity of ordinary people making, shifting or dismantling borders, an activity that leads to cosmopolitan experiences (2011: 262–4). Similarly, for Sarah Green, borderwork is 'about the way that borders appear, disappear and reappear, perhaps somewhere else, in the course of everyday life' (2013: 9). It could be argued that many contemporary films (and many that are not contemporary) are such agents of 'borderwork'. *Before Sunrise* and the trilogy are among them. Yet, what is more relevant is the centrality of borders, their visibility and their various configurations in cosmopolitan thinking. It might be said that, although in a different way from Mignolo's, border thinking is an important part of the cosmopolitan lens. This brings us directly into the fictional world of *Before Sunrise*.

Before Sunrise takes place in Vienna, relatively far from geopolitical borders. Yet, the fact that the characters are French and US American and that the people they meet in the story are mostly Austrian, means that borders arise whenever the characters interact with one another and with the city. As Mike Davis argues about Mexican migrants in a different context, cross-border travellers carry the border with them wherever they go (2000: 71), although, it must be added, some border-crossers carry them more lightly than others. As a consequence of this narrative setup, borderwork is performed throughout the narrative and the idea of the border is always implicit in the exchanges between the protagonists and theirs with the environment. The film's Vienna becomes a border city. We will focus on the importance of Vienna as cinematic and geohistorical space in the next chapter, but here we will deploy the cosmopolitan lens described above to explore the formal strategies used by the filmmakers to construct a transnational scenario.

Maria Rovisco identifies cosmopolitan cinema, if not as a genre, as a mode of production and as an aesthetic practice (2013: 154). Taking her cue from Hamid Naficy's notion of 'accented cinema' (2001), she lists certain formal characteristics of this practice: a recognisable self-reflexive and multilingual style (2013: 153), a reliance on the power of visual images, location shooting and visual imagery that challenges the idea that suffering is 'unrepresentable' (155–6). This is, more or less, a distillation of the elements characterising Naficy's 'accented style' (2006: 118–21). For us, on the other hand, there is no univocal correspondence between cosmopolitan narratives and specific cinematic forms. We are, in fact, less interested in pinpointing a category of cosmopolitan films than in viewing films, in this case, *Before Sunrise*, through a cosmopolitan lens. We explore the specific formal choices utilised by the film in order to construct its border dynamics but do not draw these choices from a pre-constituted list. This would narrow our focus excessively.

For instance, a superficial look immediately shows that *Before Sunrise* is, apart from location shooting, much closer to classical filmmaking than to the 'alternative' cinema described by Rovisco and Naficy. Both authors have in mind films about migration, diaspora and exile (Naficy actually talks of 'exilic cinema' 2001) and not narratives of white middle-class people travelling around Europe, a fact that places the film within the contradictory nature of the cosmopolitan, as we have just seen. The film may be independent within an industrial and even aesthetic US context but it is not stylistically groundbreaking or radical. Wood, for example, describes it as possessing 'a closed and perfect classical form' (1998: 325), a formal approach that the film shares with much independent cinema. Neither is the film explicitly political or socially engaged. This does not deduct from its engagement with transnational issues or from its potential to explore borders in the context of globalising processes. The cosmopolitan perspective allows us to explore whatever formal elements a film deploys in connection with borderliness, cross-border mobilities and transnational issues, rather than look for the presence of a predetermined set of features or for a category of 'cosmopolitan films'.

The Cosmopolitan Lens 2: From the Long Take to Transnational Youth Cultures

What are the film's stylistic blocks? Drawing from Wood, MacDowell describes the film's, and the trilogy's, most discussed formal choice – the long take – as striking a 'delicate balance' between classical transparency, in its apparent artless simplicity, and self-consciousness, for it encourages us to notice the dramatic action (2017: 150). The centrality of this rhetorical figure in *Before Sunrise* is closely linked to the 'walking and talking' structure of the film, with the two characters framed without cuts as they walk around Vienna, even though not all of the film's long takes show the couple walking. There are substantial long takes of the characters walking in the Prater and alongside the Donaukanal, but the two most often discussed instances of the long take – the tram ride (almost six minutes long) and the record shop booth (over two minutes) – frame the two characters sitting or standing rather than walking. Sometimes the characters are strolling around Vienna but the scenes are shot in a leisurely but classical style that employs continuity editing, as when they visit the narrow streets of Mölker Steig and Spittelberg in the city centre. Other times, as in the pinball scene or the pretend telephone conversations at Café Sperl, stationary conversations are conveyed through classically cut shot/reverse shot sequences. The film, therefore, does not draw univocal links between visual form and narrative. Long takes and shot sequences alternate in seamless ways and have different functions.

The night scene at the park, a climax of sorts, is a good example of the film's formal strategy and its use of all the above: in this case, shot/reverse shots of the two characters lying together on the grass, generally in close-up, are interspersed with various iterations of the master shot – an overhead medium shot of the two – sometimes close to a long take, with an average shot length of ten seconds, which approximates the cutting rhythm of the whole film [see Figure 4.1]. The culmination of desire here refers to an earlier scene in which Céline and Jesse had disagreed about life's priorities:

Figure 4.1 The slow pace of young love

Jesse had been reluctant to commit himself to a stable relationship that might stop him from achieving great goals in life. For Céline, on the other hand, more important than personal and professional success was 'the little space in between people', where God and magic ultimately reside: the attempt at trying to understand someone, something that may be ultimately unrealisable but is still worth living for. As a romantic comedy, the film is a cinematic articulation of this goal and the park scene the moment in which that little space is most alive, as the two characters come together physically and emotionally. But from a cosmopolitan perspective, this little space acquires a different meaning: two young people whose national and cultural difference becomes the engine of desire and, in crossing the border and opening themselves to the other, experience, in the terms proposed by Delanty, a cosmopolitan moment.

In the course of the film, and of the next two, the actors' performances and their dialogue underline their linguistic, political and cultural differences, often in terms of comic banter. Yet, national difference and cultural misunderstandings are usually downplayed in a narrative context in which transnational coexistence is more a given than something to strive for, something that is closely linked to the age of the characters and the easy-going tolerance associated with youth. The film's naturalistic style in terms of visual rhetoric and performance makes this easy, fluid border-crossing seem the most natural thing in the world (Deleyto 2019: 27). By the time they have reached the park, in the dark, softly lit and symmetrically framed, the young American man and the young French woman display more visual similarities than differences. It could, in fact, be argued that, beyond their different nationalities and maybe politics, Jesse and Céline are, from the start, not that different from each other. The film may celebrate a difference that is not all that great and, consequently, undermine its apparent unemphatic cosmopolitanism and its engagement with tolerance and diversity (31). As the characters embrace under the Vienna stars, the celebration of difference may have turned into a celebration of similarity and the kind of betrayal of cosmopolitan aspirations and ethics suggested by, among others, Fine (2006), Stacey (2017) and Mignolo (2011).

Their similarities in terms of race, class and cultural background must, then, not be underestimated. They contribute to the film's status as an instance of the ambivalence and contradictions of every day or 'actually existing' cosmopolitanism, as Robbins defines this notion (1998: 1–19). At the same time, we must recognise that their affinity is not only a matter of cultural background: the characters' age (at the cemetery, Céline says she is twenty-three and we assume Jesse's age is similar), regardless of their national origins, plays a crucial part in the carefree and unemphatic way that they approach borders, even as they often incorporate their cultural differences into their conversations. The fact that Céline and Jesse are largely two young people acting their age also affects the film's choice of formal strategies: the relative slowness of the pace and of the editing, the length of the long takes, the naturalism of the performances and the use of settings.

The rhythm of the film has been related to the concept of slacker that Linklater's earlier film had popularised as defining a generation. As discussed in Chapter 1, Stone finds intricate connections with Guy Debord's concept of *dérive* and its 'incitement to losing yourself gainfully in spaces thought to be under the control of a system' (2013: 22) but this dissenting philosophy is, as Stone claims, part of the generational outlook of the youth culture with which Linklater's films were associated. The aimlessness of the characters' itineraries, as well as the *temps mort* in which they occur, their sauntering in the streets of a foreign city that they easily make their own, correspond to a particular period in people's lives, one that, with historically specific connotations, Linklater consciously aims to capture here. In this sense, it is interesting that the plot of the film (like those of the next two) is organised around a deadline, in this case, the departure of Jesse's flight the following morning. The characters increasingly feel the pressure of their impending separation and yet constantly develop strategies to defuse that pressure, such as their pacts to say goodbye before the night is over or to not make plans to meet again. These strategies, as argued in the previous chapter, only work imperfectly in the end, but they contribute to the construction of a world in which time appears to pass slowly and potential problems may flare up but never alter the easy atmosphere created from the beginning.

In this context, slack, *dérive*, *temps mort* and Bergsonian *durée*, which sees time as fluid and what is always happening, rather than a measurable category (Stone 2013: 76), become, largely because of the protagonists' youth, a central part of the film's approach to transnational relationships. The narrative deployment of unhurried presentness and a space that is completely devoid of anxiety-producing challenges on the characters create an atmosphere in which they are free to explore and savour the other's otherness as well as their commonalities. From a cosmopolitan perspective, Linklater's philosophy of 'slack' in *Before Sunrise* may be seen as a form of cosmopolitan canopy, the term coined by Elijah Anderson for those settings that offer 'a respite from the lingering tensions of urban life and an opportunity for diverse people to come together' in which cosmopolitan attitudes are encouraged (2011: xiv, 70–1). In a sense, Jesse and Céline's youth *is* their cosmopolitan canopy. It allows them to ignore the pressures of everyday life and inspires them to reach out to the other without much heed for caution or fear of difference. Because the characters meet at a time in which they have their whole lives ahead of them and in which the fear of missing something that might never return is largely absent, barriers that would otherwise have existed fall down. Both the film's narrative scaffolding and its formal strategies contribute to the construction of this cosmopolitan canopy. Under it, both similarity and difference play into the protagonists' growing affinity and their eagerness to learn from each other, re-examine their own priorities and initiate a process of reflexive transformation even as they fall in love.

The Cosmopolitan Lens 3: Framing the Little Space

From a cosmopolitan perspective, the dynamic of similarity and difference is a central organising principle of the film, both thematically and formally. Céline's 'little space in between' delineates not only its thematic structure, both as a romantic comedy and as a transnational narrative, but also its formal approach and, specifically, its construction of filmic space. This approach becomes apparent in the film's use of frame distance, one that is determined, among other things, by the characters' age. In terms of borderwork, this is the story of two young people making the most of the borders that in separating them also bring them together. Variations in frame distance reproduce this dynamic and metaphorically delineate the scope and progression of their relationship.

The 'little space in between' dialogue takes place two thirds into the film, when spectators have already become familiar with the characters and have witnessed their growing affinity. In spatial terms, this may be considered the emotional centre of the story: as they walk through the narrow streets of the Spittelberg area, the summer evening acquires a magic quality, with the yellowish colour of the street lamps softly bathing the walls of the buildings. Gradually, the two appear to be irresistibly drawn to one another. Their conversation has fluidly turned from gender difference to the wonders and the anxieties of love. The camera follows them from a distance that fluctuates between the long and the medium shot. Then, as they sit on a bench in a conveniently empty street, they are framed in close-up. Jesse bares his soul, taking the conversation in a direction that neither spectators nor Céline were expecting, when he muses: 'if I'm totally honest with myself, I think I'd rather die knowing that I was good as something. That I had excelled in some way'. He adds that this aspiration is incompatible with commitment to another person. He is framed in close-up as, for a few seconds, he seems to have found something more important than his attraction to Céline. The tight framing may indicate that we are now reaching the core of his inner self, his deepest dream, which is worrying from both a romantic perspective and a cosmopolitan perspective.

In the subsequent reverse shot, also a close-up, Delpy's face registers Céline's disappointment at his self-involvement with a slight lowering of her eyelids. She immediately counters with the story of the older man who, at fifty-two, realised that 'he had never given anything of himself' and 'his life was for no one or nothing'. Gradually, as she explains her theory of godliness and magic, the combination of the actor's performance, her youth, her way of speaking and her gaze draw Jesse's attention and his fascination back to her and away from his own dreams of greatness. The little space visually constructed by the close-up has now switched from the individualistic to the interpersonal. At this point, the spectators have become involved in the same little space that separates the characters and draws them together, frame distance both bringing us as close as possible to their feelings and spatially replicating the distance between them. The little space between the characters becomes also the little space between us and them. Then, after one more close-up of each in silence, the sequence ends with a long shot in which not only the space between them but also the space around them becomes visible and intensely present [see Figures 4.2–4.4]. This long distance underlines their togetherness but, simultaneously, also repositions the characters in the narrow street, among the ochre buildings, the street lamps and the Vienna evening. They are not just prospective lovers but lovers in a particular space, one that both fosters their cosmopolitan openness and replicates it. The little space situates the encounter in Vienna.

This construction of the protagonists and the city through frame distance in the Spittelberg scene extends to the whole film. Some spectators may, in retrospect, feel that the camera has focused intensely on the characters, that distances have been generally short, and the city has remained out of focus in the background, just the stage for their emotional/transnational connection. Yet, the spaces that they traverse have been imprinted vividly in our minds. Most of the times Céline and Jesse kiss they are framed in close-up, but not always. For instance, their kiss at Albertinaplatz, the last before they return to the station in the morning, is framed in extreme long shot, with the visual emphasis as much on the lit-up Opera House behind them as on the two characters [see Figure 4.5]. In moments like this, even as we focus on the two central figures, we become aware of the importance of the cinematic space and of the real space that it inhabits. It is as if the text were constantly asking us to understand the inseparability between characters and place. This seems to be the purpose of an earlier transitional sequence which

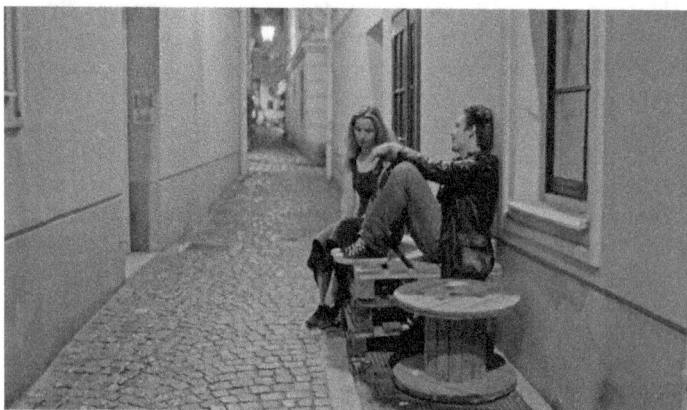

Figures 4.2–4.4 Framing the little space in between … and beyond

Figure 4.5 Kissing outside the opera

at first sight appears to be there just to convey the impression of life really lived, with its *temps mort* (see Norton 2000: 64) and apparently irrelevant conversation. In their wanderings around the city, Céline and Jesse have stopped in front of the poster of a Seurat exhibition. The canvas reproduced in the poster is 'La voie ferrée'. To Céline, who has seen the painting before, the French artist's *oeuvre* constructs a world in which the environment is stronger than the people: in his paintings, she says, humans appear to dissolve into space. This is a metaphor for the role of Vienna in the film – not the background for the action but its engine and even what the story is ultimately about. The balance between characters and city, between foreground and background, between narrative and space, is formally captured by the variations in frame distance, both close-ups and long shots and the rest of the distances in between, both conveying narrative development and the role of the city in the movie.

Vienna

Why Vienna? From a cosmopolitan perspective, the Austrian capital is at a crossroads of civilisations. Austria is *Östereich*, the eastern realm or eastern land, the meeting of east and west at the centre of the continent, an apt location for a transnational narrative because of its geographical location and its long history of many types of intercultural encounters. This dimension of the city is never underlined in the film. In the course of the story, we do not explicitly learn anything about Vienna. In fact, Jesse and Céline leave much to be desired as explorers or even tourists. Standing in a cabin of the famous Wiener Riesenrad, Céline casually mentions the Danube and points in its direction. 'That's a river, right?', answers Jesse, more interested in kissing the young woman than in a river along whose long course a great deal of European history has been played out over the centuries. They walk past Maria Theresien Platz, kiss in front of the Opera House but do not even look in its direction or at the Palais Albertina, behind them. Along the Donaukanal, around Spittelberg and in the neighbourhood of Saint Stephen's Cathedral, they are more interested in cafés to stop or benches to sit on than in the city's history. They do visit Maria am Gestade Church and spend some time sitting inside but they do not mention or, seemingly, even notice its architectural wonders.

And yet, *we* do. While those familiar enough with the city may find the liberties the filmmakers take with its geography and its constant manipulation of the distance between places frustrating, the spectators' immersion in the real spaces of the Austrian capital is intense. We may choose to ignore it but, as Rhodes and Gorfinkel remind us, our experience of the cinema is intimately connected with the experience of place because of the medium's potential to record place (2011: viii–ix). From a different perspective, space is, for Antoine Gaudin, an organising force in a film and something that engages spectators at the deepest level (2015: 200). *Before Sunrise* confirms this centrality of space in the cinema and openly invites viewers to meditate on the places it records even as it transforms them through formal work and narrative incident. What we make of the film's Vienna depends on each individual viewer. For a critic, it will revolve around her particular approach to the film. In our case, looking through a cosmopolitan lens, we will describe the city as it appears in *Before Sunrise* as a synecdoche for Europe and as the location of the renewed European project that was gathering pace when the film came out. In this, the youth of the characters becomes both a metaphor of the 'young Europe' being imagined at the time and, however modestly, an engine of its development. We devote the next chapter to the exploration of this dimension of the film.

5 Europe 95

Cinema and the Real World

In a brief contribution to a book on cinema and the city, which constitutes a lament for early filmmaking before the medium developed strategies to 'control cinema' to the detriment of 'the outside world', Geoffrey Nowell-Smith finds two general types of city films: those that are mostly studio-shot and those that are mostly location-shot, with various gradations between them. There is, among the latter, a core of films that provide a strong sense of place as a result of the link between the film setting and the actual location. However, the most interesting cases for him are those which may not be openly about the city but in which the city conditions the fiction 'by its recalcitrance and its inability to be subordinated to the demands of the narrative' (2001: 104). Here he mentions cases like Naples in Roberto Rossellini's *Journey to Italy* (1954) – which, incidentally, will be an important intertext in *Before Midnight* – and Milan in Michelangelo Antonioni's *La Notte* (1961). Antonioni's cities specifically 'are there before they signify, and they signify because they are there' (107), that is, their meanings predate the film. The author is calling our attention to the importance of the real world (he writes about cities, but the same could be said of other real places) in the cinema – not only how films may articulate meanings about that real world but, more crucially, how important that real world becomes in the films themselves – an infiltration of reality in the filmic fiction. This is a reality that filmmakers cannot fully control but one which they may or may not choose to embrace. Most, for Nowell-Smith, do not, and, in not embracing the real world, they miss the chance of learning from it.

Something similar may be said about film spectators and critics. Films in which location shooting predominates and in which the real places are recognisable and explicitly referred to, like the *Before* films, allow spectators to immerse themselves in those places, an outside world that has become part not only of the fiction but also of the mise-en-scène – the world turned into film form. This real world, which is there and remains there after the film has passed through it, resists any narrative transformations that formal strategies may subject it to. Thus, the film, beyond its particular narrative dynamics, becomes a half-open door to the real world, and the mise-en-scène

DOI: 10.4324/9781003224334-6

an interface between text and reality. This is an interface that spectators are free, sometimes encouraged, to navigate, even if it means straying away from the fictional world constructed by the movie.

Geographer Doreen Massey argues that space does not exist in absolute terms – it is linked to time and history. It is, in her definition, a simultaneity of stories-so-far (2005: 24). We perceive space through narratives. Our understanding of a place is the aggregate of all the microhistories that have occurred in it and all the stories that have been told about it. By opening the cinematic text to the real locations; by, in a sense, losing themselves in the real world and losing partial control over the tools of signification, some films invite us to consider and explore the history of the place and to contextualise the fictional story and its meanings within it. If we look closely, we will find clues to that history everywhere on the surface of the text that may guide us on our journey around its peripheries.

Nowell-Smith concludes his chapter by underlining the importance of the real materials filmmakers work with, materials that retain their original quality regardless of how much the film's formal and narrative work transforms them. This is 'a privilege which filmmakers neglect at their peril' (2001: 107). Likewise with spectators. In his theory of film space, Gaudin affirms that in the cinema we do not only see represented spaces but *experience* space, an experience that makes filmic space real. Film space is a lived space – lived because experienced by the spectator (2015: 54, 200). He, therefore, locates the experience of film space not so much in the film itself, not so much in the hands of the filmmakers, but in the spectator. While Gaudin's real space is the whole of cinematic space as such and not just the real space that has infiltrated the film, it can equally be argued that the activation of real places when we watch a film is also the responsibility of the spectator and the critic.

A Contemporary European Space

Rosalind Galt has argued convincingly that in the early 1990s, Europe became a question of space, following the fall of the Berlin Wall and the reunification of Germany, the break-up of the Soviet Union and the breakdown of Yugoslavia. For the first time since World War II, the borders were unstable and then in the 1990s, the European Union expanded to incorporate new members, including Austria. With this background, Galt sets out to explore the ways in which European cinema represented these revisions of European space (2006: 1). *Before Sunrise*, although not industrially a European film, and its two sequels are part of this contemporary meditation on European space. We would like to argue that the trilogy delineates its own account of this period in which space became crucial for the continent. Its way of engaging with this space follows Nowell-Smith's account of the impact of real places in certain films. Although the narrative apparently focuses on the encounter and growing romance between Jesse and Céline, extended location shooting puts the story in the 'special' category of films like *La Notte*, *Journey to Italy* and the neorealist films mentioned by Nowell-Smith. This is, in the first place, the Vienna that we see in the film: the streets, the buildings, the squares and the canals, as well as the people that Céline and Jesse interact with. Through them, it is also, crucially, the Masseyan Vienna: the simultaneity of stories-so-far that those real places contain underneath the surface, the history that they evoke by their mere presence and 'reality'. That is, the geographical space that installs itself within the film's textuality is also a place with a long history, none of which is, potentially, completely outside the film and can therefore be 'recalled' as part of the filmic text. Textual and contextual factors encourage viewers to tease out parts of this history. This is also a version of what, after Henri Lefebvre (1991), geographers and cultural critics denominate social space: a space that is socially produced through discourse and social practices, as well as cultural practices. We might say that, per Nowell-Smith, the real Vienna is not only there and signifies because it is there, but also that, in being visited by *Before Sunrise* and subjected to the cultural work performed by the film, it becomes something ever so slightly different from before; or, at least, certain historical, cultural and social dimensions of the city are brought to the fore and are elaborated upon through the film's intervention. The film becomes one more of the stories-so-far that make up the space of Vienna.

Simultaneously, given the historical moment in which the film was released and in which the action takes place, and given the locations and historical moments of the two sequels – Paris nine years later in *Before Sunset* and the southern Peloponnese another nine years on in *Before Midnight* – the real space of the film and the trilogy becomes the larger space of Europe, as defined by the European Union, of the 1990s through the 2010s. It may, therefore, be surmised that, in the films' cultural imagination, this European canvas is inscribed in history and it starts in Vienna, precisely in the year in which Austria would join the European Union. Together, through their deployment of this social space and their open door to the real world, the three films offer a remarkable panorama of the process of transnational European integration in the course of the three decades in which they were released. We argue that, in a more historically specific form than, for instance the Spanish *Lovers of the Arctic Circle* (Medem 1998) in Galt's interpretation, Linklater's movie textualises European transnational space (2006: 106). This spatial dimension constitutes an important part of the significance and power of the trilogy: a chronicle of contemporary Europe, from early ambitions of progress towards political union, through the growing tide of nationalist retrenchment and magnification of internal and external differences, to the onset of a crisis that, starting in 2008, still shows no signs of abating. The trilogy's consistent deployment of real space refers to this historical reality, even as the parallels between it and the narrative of intimacy proliferate.

The story, then, begins in Vienna. As in the films mentioned by Nowell-Smith, Vienna is everywhere to be seen in *Before Sunrise* but, in case we have, at our own peril, failed to notice it, engrossed as we may have been by the romantic story happening in the foreground, the filmmakers remind us of the importance of the 'real mise-en-scène' of the film in the often-mentioned montage sequence that precedes the final two shots. Linked, as discussed in Chapter 2, by the slow-moving notes and wandering harmonies of Bach's sonata to the farewell scene at the railway station and the final two shots of Jesse and Céline resuming their individual journeys to, respectively, the US and Paris, this sequence lasts seventy-five seconds and is composed of ten shots of the places the characters have visited in the course of the narrative. These include the Zollamtssteg Bridge, the boat café on the Donaukanal, Albertina and the Opera House, the bench in Spittelberg where Céline introduces the little space in between, the Cemetery of the Unnamed, the Prater Ferris Wheel, the Kleines Café on Franziskanerplatz and the park where they lay on the grass [see Figures 3.1–3.3 in Chapter 3]. Except that these places are now (almost) empty and the background has become the totality of the frame. Critics have read this scene in different ways. For instance, Wood, taking the famous final scene of *L'Eclisse* (1962) as a referent, finds that, where Antonioni's sequence evoked desolation and finality, Linklater's suggests happiness and sadness intermingled (1998: 334). It could be argued that it is the magic of the city – the mysteries and wonders of the real Vienna as captured and selected in the film – that has changed the young couple, and us through them, and transported them and us to the ideal world conjured up by Bach's piece.

Bracketed as it is by narrative incident, the sequence remains immersed in the story, prompting spectators to interpret it as part of the narrative, but, in a different sense, it reminds spectators of a city for which the story is already in the past and, consequently, of the importance of the city itself, now devoid of the presence of the characters to distract our attention. Or, we might say that in *Before Sunrise*, Jesse and Céline are ultimately signifiers of Vienna, much like the human figures in Seurat's paintings. It is to this real Vienna and to its identity as a European city that we now turn our attention. We said above that in the trilogy, Europe starts in Vienna, but it would be more accurate to say that, in purely chronological and spatial terms, it starts before Vienna: it starts on a train bound for Vienna and Paris. This train, together with the presence of the Danube River, openly situate the film's locations as part of a larger trans-European reality. It is for this reason that the analysis that follows will start with the railway and end with the river.

On the Train 1: Travelling around Europe

Céline, a young woman from Paris, and Jesse, an American visiting Europe, cross paths on the train from Budapest to Paris. In 1995, such an encounter would have seemed anything but far-fetched. The interrail pass had been introduced in 1972 for under twenty-one-year-olds, covering twenty-one European countries; but had, by the time of the film, been expanded to people under twenty-six (as well as to senior citizens) and to twenty-nine countries. But if interrail made it easier for young people to travel around the continent and contributed to visualising late twentieth-century Europe as a space of young people crossing borders, a more far-reaching scheme was the establishment of the Erasmus student exchange programme, as part of the supranational institution's political transition from a 'common market' to a 'union'.

Erasmus was created in 1987 to foster trans-border mobility among European students and, as a consequence, a sense among the continent's youth of being part of a multinational body. In his book on *L'auberge espagnol* (Klapisch 2002) for the Cinema and Youth Cultures series, Ben McCann elaborates on the importance, as well as the shortcomings and contradictions, of Erasmus as a European project. He explains the programme's ultimate goal as one of fighting 'walled-off nationalism and xenophobia' and encouraging a shared awareness of national and supranational identity among those who would eventually become the adult European citizens of the twenty-first century (2018: 37). Some figures quoted by McCann speak for themselves: 3.3 million exchange students all over Europe by the programme's thirtieth anniversary in 2017, around twenty-five per cent of Erasmus students having met their long-term partners while on exchange, and over a million 'Erasmus babies' having been born as a result by 2014. This 'Erasmus generation' constituted a new generation of European citizens, eager to 'internalize a European consciousness' (38). Not that Erasmus appeared out of the blue. Vincenzo Cicchelli places it within the centuries-old historical context of European travel, with precedents in the lower Middle Ages, when the first universities were created, and, in the late eighteenth century, with voyages around the continent, particularly to Italy and Greece, constituting one of the preferred means to complete the education of children of the dominant classes (2013: 1). The enthusiasm with which students from around Europe, particularly from Italy, Spain, France, Germany and the UK, took to the programme often contrasted with the reticence and growing resistance of national political institutions and often populations at large to move forward towards the goal of a more united Europe.

Céline is not an Erasmus student but, as a twenty-three-year-old student of La Sorbonne, she may have easily been one in the recent past. In any case, her evident familiarity with travel abroad, including stays in Los Angeles and London, places her within the cultural logic of European travel among the young that received a definitive boost from Erasmus. In 1995 she would have been one of thousands of men and women in their early twenties moving around Europe and coming into contact with young people from other countries. She meets Jesse, a young US man about the same age, also a college student at some point, travelling around the continent on an interrail pass.

Although he initially says that, after the fiasco of his visit to Madrid, he had bought the cheapest flight back to the US, which happened to leave from Vienna two or three weeks later, he then changes his version, confessing that he could not face returning home straight away after the break-up. Whatever the reason, the narrative has created this *temps mort* for him to aimlessly ride trains, apparently not enjoying the experience, except of course, in the last day before departing when he meets Céline and his few hours in Vienna force him to change his mind.

Americans in Europe have been a frequent presence in the history of Hollywood cinema, from *An American in Paris* (Minnelli 1951) to *Mamma Mia!* (Lloyd 2008), from *One, Two, Three* (Wilder 1961) to *Vicky Cristina Barcelona* (Allen 2008), from *Roman Holiday* (Wyler 1953) to *The Bourne Identity* (Liman 2002) and its sequels. For Stone, however, the 'Europeanness' of *Before Sunrise* is more intense than in other cases: it is the film's literary and philosophical sensibilities that define its links to European culture (2007: 225). The film focuses equally on both protagonists (rather than mostly on the American) and Céline's awakening to the possibility of catharsis through her relationship with Jesse reveals 'a European sensibility' (226). For Stone, there are interesting parallels between the slacker mentality and 'the cool flavour of the French New Wave' in its structure, characters and themes, while Céline is, in cinematic terms, a child of the *nouvelle vague* (221, 224). From Jesse's perspective, it could be argued that his engagement with European culture, through the intensity of his time with Céline and through their joint 'slacking' or *dérive* in Vienna, also imbues him with the beginnings of a hybrid sensibility that, unbeknown to him at this point (and to contemporary spectators at the time), will change his life. It might be argued that the film embodies the slacker worldview specific to US independent cinema in the early 1990s and, through its parallels and intersections with European cultural and, specifically, cinematic trends, finds its passage into a culturally hybrid and outsider form of European cinema.

Stone's general point is about the fertile common ground between American and European cinema created by *Before Sunrise* and *Before Sunset* (234 and *passim*). We would like to argue the same point in a slightly different way: from a European perspective, one that is warranted by the geography and the history of the trilogy, the cultural hybridity of the films enhances the Europeanness of the fictional world created by this US independent film. Jesse does not become a European citizen and remains recognisably 'American' in his ways, although he will in time become a European resident but, in becoming the product of a hybrid experience, he contributes centrally to the trilogy's unobtrusive perspective on the vicissitudes of the continent in the course of three decades. As the trilogy progresses, he comes close to a latter-day iteration of Henry James and the European cosmopolitanism with which the nineteenth-century writer strongly identified (Figes 2019: 387). Jesse turns, in his relationship with Céline and in his manner of 'being' in Europe, into a signifier of the borderwork, border-crossing and border resistances that have been central to the recent history of the continent, both in its lofty cosmopolitan aspirations and its often less than ideal cosmopolitan realities.

James MacDowell mentions the Austrian couple whose argument on the train enables Céline and Jesse's encounter, and reminds us of how, eighteen years later, our protagonists are in danger of becoming a version of them during their protracted argument in the hotel room in *Before Midnight* (2021a: 48–9). Yet, in spite of personal ups and downs which shrewdly reflect the ups and downs of the European project, the films remain strongly committed to a comic vision, as we will argue in the final chapter. This comic perspective is already in place before the train arrives in Vienna and is, as we have seen, closely related to what we might call the Erasmus imagination. Even though not literally Erasmus students, not even students at a European university in the case of Jesse, the couple are, as a cultural construction, part of this imagination and of the cosmopolitan potential that this imagination reinforced as one of the founding principles of the European Union. Céline and Jesse are young people in a young, or rejuvenated, Europe. Their activation of national difference as the engine of desire and coexistence parallels the Union's aspirations of turning internal and external borders into connecting tissue rather than loci of exclusion and violence. The subsequent obstacles brought about by the everyday realities of these two border crossers will replicate, on a fictional and intimate sphere, the crises of the political project, a situation with which Europe continues to grapple. In geopolitical terms, neither the cosmopolitan aspirations nor the subsequent resistances and obstacles are without precedents in the history of the continent. In order to trace this genealogy, we must remain on the train for a while.

On the Train 2: A Story of Nineteenth-Century Cosmopolitanism and Nationalism

Orlando Figes places the development of the railways in Europe around the mid-nineteenth century at the centre of the creation of a European culture – 'a space of cultural transfers, translations and exchanges crossing national boundaries' (2019: 4), a cosmopolitan culture shared by the intellectual and artistic élites that spread to the middle-classes with the origins of modern tourism, also as a direct consequence of the railways. While the second half of the nineteenth century is often identified as the age of the rise of nationalisms on the continent, what is less known is that these nationalisms were, to some extent, a reaction to the earlier wave of internationalist sentiment and cosmopolitan ideals (239–40). What Figes calls 'the railway age' was the first period of cultural globalisation. It is, therefore, significant that in a transnational story with cosmopolitan aspirations set in Europe one and a half centuries later, Céline and Jesse should meet on a train.

Figure 5.1 Looking back at the cosmopolitanism of 'the railway age'

Their encounter takes place in the first few minutes of the film and is sparked by the argument of the Austrian couple in the same coach, but before the action proper starts with Jesse striking a conversation with Céline across the aisle, the credit sequence includes a series of shots of the railway that starts with a fast tracking shot of the rail tracks as the train hurries along, coinciding with the title credit [see Figure 5.1]. In other words, our first impression is that we are about to see a film called *Before Sunrise* related to the experience of train travelling. Subsequent shots feature views of the countryside from train windows, a bridge that the train crosses, a river, probably the Danube, again from the train window, and, finally, a long shot of a young woman walking along the aisle of a train car and going inside one of the compartments. Over these shots in the soundtrack, we hear a fragment from the overture of Henry Purcell's *Dido and Aeneas*. Robin Wood has suggested that the presence of Purcell's mini-opera, like the evocation of *Letter from an Unknown Woman* (Ophüls 1948) through the Vienna locations, are references to stories of romantic love that, unlike the one in the film, end tragically (1998: 325–6). He also mentions, in passing, how the beginning of the *allegro* coincides with the fade-in to the railway tracks and the passing train, aptly highlighting the kinetic quality of the moment (325), even though the story that is about to commence will develop at a much slower pace. For Cenciarelli, the closing scene, to the tune of the *andante* of Bach's piece, thematises movement (2018: 6).

As a signifier of the growth of the railways in the mid-nineteenth century, the musical reference to Purcell, from 150 years earlier, is conspicuously inaccurate but the piece does introduce the exhilaration of train travel forcefully. This is the first instance of the alternation of classical and popular music, old and new, that makes up the film's soundtrack. Purcell is the first of the classical composers that are used in the film and is followed later by Vivaldi, Beethoven and, as we have already seen, Johann Strauss and Bach. All of these references add a vague, atemporal quality to the story, which parallels the connotations of Vienna as an old European city. This is a story about the present, told, as it were, in the present tense, but the presence of the past is constantly highlighted. As discussed above, the film keeps inviting us to walk through the open door of its 'real mise-en-scène' and the classical music in the soundtrack contributes to the invitation. At the same time, the soundtrack also includes contemporary music, both local and international, that reminds us of the Vienna of the film's present. This is, therefore, not just a story about the past, like *Letter from an Unknown Woman*, but one about the influence of history in the present.

Both in the credit sequence and the first scene proper, the past that is conjured up is the impact of railway travel, not just in Vienna but in the whole of Europe. This is a past, as Figes reminds us, of the weakening of borders between countries. In the 1840s, railway lines were open between Antwerp and Cologne, from Paris to Brussels, from the French capital to Calais, and from there, by steamer boat, to England. France was soon linked to Switzerland, Bavaria to Saxony and Prussia. The Austro-Hungarian Empire had a railway from Vienna to Prague and soon built a line to Trieste, their only seaport (2019: 39–40). By the 1860s it was possible to travel by train to nearly all of Europe's major cities (218). This staggering growth brought along a sense of being 'European' bound up with the outwardlookingness that came along with international travel: the feeling of being part of Europe was connected to the possibility of travelling by rail to any part of it (237-8). In the mid-1990s, travel has changed in unforeseen ways, with roads and air travel taking precedence over the railways as the most popular ways of moving around the continent. But this film, with one eye on the present and the other on the past, as much in the story it tells as in the way of telling it, chooses to stick to the railways; a reminder of earlier spectacular border crossings at a time when crossing borders as a way to bring countries together has become part of the agenda of a new Europe.

The opening sequence, with its generic shots of train travel, its views from windows but no characters looking through them, iron bridges, central European landscapes and, probably, the Danube, is set outside the narrative. As soon as we move to the train containing the Austrian couple, Céline, Jesse and the other passengers, the music stops and the story starts. It is therefore tempting to see this sequence as an invitation to ponder the general significance of the railway, its historical beginnings and its links to the present of the continent. The bracketing of the Vienna narrative within the context of trans-European train travel reinforces the Europeanness of the film and the border crossings that were at the heart of the European project. It is therefore not just Vienna but its historical importance as a crossroads in Central Europe that *Before Sunrise* brings to the fore through location shooting and now, soundtrack. After all, Jesse and Céline will only spend a few hours in the Austrian capital. They remain people on the move, only temporarily coming together *en route* to their respective destinations. They not only spend most of their time in Vienna walking and talking. But they are also engaged in larger forms of mobility, Jesse at the end of his roaming around the continent and on his way back to the US and Céline returning home to Paris from Budapest.

Claudio Magris, as he starts his journey along the Danube, describes the feeling: 'one stares out of the window of the train as it hurtles into the country-side, one raises one's face to the breezes, and something passes, flows through the body' (2017: 15). This form of exhilaration, familiar to so many travel-lers, is harnessed by the filmmakers as a distillation of a cultural project that is larger than but also parallel with its love story. Or, to put it a different way, it is both essential for the kindling of desire between the young characters and metaphorised by it: sexual desire as a metaphor of cosmopolitan desire. *Before Sunrise* imagines its protagonists as products of the Erasmus imagina-tion, and as young people on the move who become active agents of the con-struction of a new social and cultural European space, one with strong roots in the past but projected towards an uncertain but, at that time, hopeful future. That Jesse, an American, becomes part of the equation gives a measure of the fascination of the project.

'An der schönen blauen Donau'

The title of Johann Strauss the Younger's most famous of waltzes has become almost a synonym of Vienna in the popular imagination, as millions around the world are reminded every first of January from the Viennese Musikverein concert hall in the New Year Concert. The brief sight of the river in the credit sequence of *Before Sunrise* invokes this identifica-tion. We will return to the Danube in the final part of this section. For the moment, let us follow Céline and Jesse as they get off the train and begin their walk around the Austrian capital. The two start their walk together on Zollamtssteg Bridge, where, behind the characters, we see a city of train lines, waterways and nineteenth-century buildings. The building we see behind them most of the time is the site of the University of Applied Arts, a prestigious institution where artists like Gustav Klimt, Oskar Kokoschka and others were once teachers or students. However, the two young Austrian men that they approach on the bridge, exhibiting what may be construed as a form of local humour, immediately declare that 'museums are not that funny anymore these days'. Céline asks about exhibitions but they, instead, sug-gest an amateur play in which they are both involved [See Figures 5.2–5.3]. As soon as Vienna is described as a place of classical culture, a more modern version of the city is brought up.

This dynamic is emphasised a few minutes later when the protagonists visit the Alt & Neu Teuchtler record store, a classic establishment still standing,

Figures 5.2–5.3 Vienna: a crucible of the old and the new

which literally describes itself as a combination of old and new, in this case, classical and popular music. As they peruse the racks of vinyls, the song playing is 'Dancing with da Rats', by British band Loud, but Jesse and Céline select an LP by US singer Kath Bloom for the listening booth. Inside the booth they listen to 'Come Here', a song that, like a Bach's sonata later, is singled out by the soundtrack as it bleeds into and becomes the sonic background to the next brief scene. This shows the characters walking on Maria-Theresien-Platz, past the Maria Theresa statue, the Kunsthistorisches Museum and the Naturhistorisches Museum, with detailed shots of one of the four fountains of tritons and naiads that decorate the square and of the statue of Eros and Psyche at the front of the first of the museums [see Figures 5.4–5.6]. There, they catch a tram that will take them, improbably, to the Friedhof der Namenlosen. The booth scene, which has been analysed in detail by MacDowell in a comparative analysis with a scene from Vicente Minnelli's *The Clock* (1945) (2008), constitutes an important step in the growing attraction between the two characters, a kind of choreography of the looks in one of the most reduced spaces of the film. It is also a privileged example of the false simplicity of Linklater's brand of realism and of the contribution of the performances to the film's overall design.

But in terms of the real city, it is the subsequent superimposition of Bloom's love song to the historical sites that the characters visit that is striking: the soundtrack not only reinforces the function of the images of love and desire of the statues as metonymies of the feelings beginning to develop between the protagonists but it also prompts us to look at the late nineteenth-century art through a contemporary eye, one that, like Jesse, is conspicuously American. One of the most important art history museums in Europe, the Kunsthistorisches Museum was, like the square, built at the end of the 1880s and inaugurated in 1891 under Emperor Franz Joseph I, the last of the Habsburg dynasty of the Austro-Hungarian Empire. As with other locations of the film, it signifies the grandeur and cultural sophistication of the Viennese *fin de siècle* but also, inevitably, its impending doom and its place in the setting in motion of events leading to the beginning of World War I, two decades later. In this brief scene, rather than loaded with the weight of history, the site appears light and airy, as framed through new eyes, those of the young transnational couple for whom it becomes part of the *temps mort* of their Viennese experience.

As with the dialectic between classical Viennese art and amateur theatre of the bridge scene, and the evocative name of the record store, *Before Sunrise* continues here to construct a city in which heritage and modernity are fused into a single unit. This is often self-consciously underlined in humorous ways, as when Jesse starts his Q&A game in the tram by asking Céline about her first sexual feelings, imitating the type of exaggerated central European accent often associated with Viennese psychoanalysts in Hollywood films. The linguistic parody openly evokes the figure of Sigmund Freud, another product of nineteenth-century Viennese culture with global reach. By parodying Freud as part of his game of seduction, Jesse both acknowledges the Viennese past which he and Céline now easily inhabit *and* identifies himself and his friend as a rejuvenated version of that past. In the film, nineteenth-century Vienna is often seen from a modern perspective in humorous ways or, as in the Marie-Theresien Platz scene discussed above, in ways that undercut its solemnity, but the admiration and sense of wonder remain obvious. This is a new Vienna, as it is a new Europe, as seen through the eyes of a young couple, but one in which the continuity with the past is never broken, one, in fact, in which the continuity with the past *is* the point.

Figures 5.4–5.6 From 'Come Here' to Maria-Theresien-Platz

Sometimes, instead of ironic distance, we get metacinematic references, often, up to that point, to the two most popular films about the city in English: *Letter from an Unknown Woman* and *The Third Man* (Reed 1949). The ill-fated love story of the former title hovers over *Before Sunrise* (see Wood's extensive comparison 1998: 325–8), not the least during the long scene at the Prater and the Riesenrad. The amusement park and its Ferris wheel are also remembered by film fans from their presence in *The Third Man* but another moment of *Before Sunrise* is perhaps more interesting in relation to Carol Reed's movie. As they wander around the narrow streets of the city centre, the couple pass by Schreyvogelgasse, the street where Harry Lime (Orson Welles) makes his unforgettable appearance in *The Third Man*. Here Linklater, the film buff, purposefully pays homage to the older film and, in doing so, places his own movie as part of the same tradition. The spot is, in fact, only a few steps away from one of several houses where Beethoven lived during his thirty-five years in Vienna, currently occupied by a souvenir shop of the German musician (Billock 2020).

As Céline and Jesse stroll leisurely along the narrow street, the worlds of Orson Welles and Beethoven come together in the cultural imaginary of the film, as their stories do in the space of the city. Most spectators will not be aware of the historical links of the narrow street and yet the juxtaposition of the classical and the popular, or, in a different sense, of classicism in an older and a newer art, of nineteenth- and twentieth-century Viennese culture, are there. More generally, the links between past and present or, in this case, a more distant and a closer past, are part of the film's discourse. The real space makes this discourse richer and more layered. Underscoring the constant parallels and contrasts is their common denominator: the evocation of a trans-European sensibility and culture as a necessary precedent for the renewed aspirations of Europeanness chronicled by the film and the trilogy.

The combination of this historical imagination based on the real city and the two foreigners fleshes out within a historical framework the transnational character of the filmic space that was discussed in Chapter 4: Vienna as a place of historical transnational and multinational credentials. Claudio Magris refers to a sixteenth-century poem by Wolfgang Schmetzl that compares Vienna to Babel, a city in which one hears people speaking Hebrew, Greek, Latin, German, French, Turkish, Spanish, Bohemian, Slovenian, Italian, Hungarian, Dutch, Syrian, Croatian, Serbian, Polish and Chaldean (2017: 176). It is also a city that lies at the centre of the continent and one that culturally and historically looks to the East as much as to the West – from a Western European perspective, a gate to the East. For Magris, the city encapsulates the many-nationed crucible of the Austro-Hungarian Empire (194), a city that is a crossroads, 'a place of departures and returns, of people, both celebrated and obscure, whom history gathers together and then disperses, in the vagabond impermanence that is our destiny' (216). This melancholy past is picked up by Jesse and Céline as they become imbued by the spirit of the city. Their presence in Vienna becomes one more iteration of the departures and returns and of manifold intersections determined by the historical spatiality of the city. At the same time, it might be said, the crossroads that is the city eventually becomes embodied in the film's protagonists: in Jesse and Céline, the history of tolerance, hybrid identities and everyday transnational occurrences repeats itself once more. One of the things that we see through the open door of location shooting is a series of lessons for the present, models to be followed.

Mitteleuropa: Core and Periphery

Which brings us back to the Danube. In Strauss's famous waltz as in many other cultural manifestations, the river is often identified with Vienna, but the Danube is a much larger geographical and cultural entity. Location shooting acknowledges the presence of the river, as we have already suggested earlier in this chapter. Therefore, it may be said that the Danube is also part of the real world that becomes incorporated into the film's narrative. *Before Sunrise* never emphasises its presence but the river is nevertheless there from the opening scene. The Friedhof der Namenlosen, which Jesse and Céline visit early in their wanderings, is located on the bank of the river and, although we do not actually see it, Céline explains that 'the nameless' refers to anonymous people whose bodies were found floating in it. From the top of the Prater's Wiener Riesenrad, Céline points at the Danube, which we again do not see, and Jesse, as part of his performance of the dumb American, asks whether that is the name of a river. Later, in one of the central, longest scenes, the couple walk along the Donaukanal, the southernmost of the four watercourses that today are called 'Danube' and were once part of a riverine landscape that spanned more than six kilometres in width (Winiwarter, Schmid and Dressel 2013). This is where they meet the street poet who writes the 'milk shake' poem for them but it is also a scene in which they start imagining themselves as a couple. We find them back at the Donaukanal later, this time at a boat café. Here the inevitability of separation is becoming real and they make the decision, later reversed, not to get in touch again. As they reach their tentative decision, Strauss is heard in the background, played by two street musicians, as discussed before. The relationship is becoming something unique and the film ensures that the location is part of that uniqueness: Vienna as a borderland in which such rare things may happen.

This café and the river reappear in the final montage sequence, now empty [See Figures 5.7–5.8]. While the structure of the story precludes the narrative from venturing down the waters of this most transnational of European rivers, *Before Sunrise* seems, from its credit sequence to its final moments, to acknowledge its importance in any story set in Vienna. The Danube is an explicit signifier of Europe: it flows from the Black Forest in southern Germany to the Black Sea, its delta, the largest in the European Union,

Figures 5.7–5.8 The Danube: European history as mise-en-scène

straddling the coasts of Romania and Ukraine. At 2,850 km, it is the second longest river in Europe after the Volga in Russia, but, unlike the Volga, it runs through ten different countries, the largest number for a river in the world. On its way it passes through cities like Ulm, Linz, Bratislava, Budapest, Belgrade and, of course, Vienna. First published in 1986, Claudio Magris's *Danube* contrasts this river with the Rhine: the Danube is the river along which 'different peoples meet and mingle and crossbreed' while the Rhine evokes the purity of the race. The Danube represents the Austria of the Habsburgs and its 'multiple, supranational culture, an Austro-Hungarian Empire formed by a community of "peoples" whose national anthem was sung in eleven different languages' (2017: 29). In the course of history, it became the crucible of many nations. When the Austro-Hungarian Empire collapsed at the end of the World War I, it left a feeling of not belonging anywhere but also that 'that elusive identity […] was not simply the destiny of the children of the Danube but a general historical condition, the being of each and every individual' (194). It thus evokes a Europe in which national identity may one day be of secondary importance, even though, as Galt argues for the 1990s, the notion of a trans-European identity is as desired in certain quarters as it is felt to be impossible (2006: 104).

However, the Danube does not encompass a whole continent. A large part of Europe falls outside its influence. Something similar may be said about the cosmopolitan Europeanness that, according to Figes, was brought to the fore by the expansion of the railways in the nineteenth century. This was a Europeanness with conspicuous limitations. Magris associates the Danube with the idea of *Mitteleuropa*, through its connections, first, with the Holy Roman Empire and, then, with the Austro-Hungarian Empire. For Magris, the river evokes nostalgia for the civilising impact of a transnational Central Europe, particularly in the later days of the Habsburg Empire (2017: 29), when Trieste was one of the most important cities and the only commercial port of the Empire. Figes, for his part, affirms that, as border crossings intensified, by the mid-nineteenth century a distinct cultural map of Europe had emerged, with a 'core' in France, the Low Countries and the German lands, and a periphery, from Spain to the Black Sea, what European writers of the time referred to as 'the internal Orient' (2019: 68). A century later, the European Economic Community that was created after the Treaty of Rome in 1957, originated, approximately, from the same core. The later process of political integration, which was officially ratified at the Treaty of Maastricht in 1992, started from the same region.

Magris's *Mitteleuropa* and Figes's core Europe do not completely coincide geographically but may be said to overlap to a great extent and to point at hierarchies and degrees of Europeanness. As the union grew, social, political and economic differences among member states became more urgent and visible, and the threat of dissolution more palpable and durable. The rift between North and South, which some historians trace back to the tenth century (Ruiz-Domènec 2022: 90), came to the fore in the crisis of 2008 whereas tensions between West and East have continued to flare up as Eastern European countries joined the union. The core/periphery dialectic goes some way towards explaining the spatial and geopolitical configurations of recent European history and the complexities of European integration, but it is, as we can see, a much older debate. Inevitably, it has transpired into various forms of European cinema (Konstantarakos 2000: 4). This irregular geography is also implicit in *Before Sunrise*, with Parisian Céline and Anglo Jesse meeting in one of the capitals of *Mitteleuropa*. The characters' similar physical appearance, their relaxed attitude towards crossing borders and even their process of falling in love, reveal, from a European perspective, their proximity and that of the film's space to the historical core of the continent (see Deleyto 2019). Of the characters they come across during their stay, the two that most openly differ from Céline and Jesse are the palm-reader and the street dancer, both vaguely reminiscent in their appearance and behaviour of the exoticism associated with the South and 'the Orient'.

At the same time, the history of Austria, the course of the Danube and the geographical location of the empire of which, until its dissolution as a consequence of World War I, Vienna remained the capital, looks towards the East. The streets of the real city along which Céline and Jesse tread lightly, often oblivious to their surroundings, also preserve this dimension as the location of a century-long cultural and historical crossroads. In the year of Austria's incorporation to the European Union, the real space of *Before Sunrise* also suggests this narrative of new beginnings. The energy and utopianism of youth is harnessed as a signifier of transnational potential, while the culturally elitist profile of the protagonists suggests the limitations and crises ahead. In Vienna, as in so many other places, the stories-so-far are endless, often contradictory, seldom homogeneous. Through the open door to the real world of the location shooting, the film gives spectators access to those stories we wish to activate but, at the same time, encourages us to make sense of them from a particular perspective, one which, as we have seen, is not devoid of contradictions, among other reasons because geography and history themselves abound in such contradictions.

Céline and Jesse represent, then, a racially homogeneous, culturally elitist, type of cosmopolitanism. In this, the angle that *Before Sunrise* and, later, the other two instalments of the trilogy offer on the recent history of Europe is at the same time limited and largely representative of the tensions and internal hierarchies that have characterised political and cultural debates around the notion of Europeanness. Together with the Paris of *Before Sunset* and the southern Peloponnese of *Before Midnight*, the film delineates a particular European space as it was being constructed in the course of three decades. Through the ostensible focus on heterosexual love and the small history of a particular couple, the films tell a story of youth progressing to adulthood that becomes enmeshed with a parallel, if in many ways not comparable, development of the idea of Europe, its ups and downs, its constant tensions and its enduring potential, its aspirations and its crises. The story of intimacy and the real spaces of Europe, narrative development and location shooting, combine in ways that can only be accessed if we as spectators accept the invitation to walk into the real world evoked by location shooting. The combination proves irresistible. Stories of youth seldom seemed more relevant than in the adventure that starts on the train to Vienna and takes its first steps in the capital of the old realm of the East.

6   Comedy and (Lost) Youth

(Just) Before Sunset at the Cradle of Comedy

In Vienna, god and magic reside in the little space between people like Céline and Jesse, as they and we marvel at the youthful desire growing between them. Eighteen years later, we find the two young lovers, now a not-so-young couple, looking at the sea and marvelling at the sunset in the coastal town of Pylos in the southern Peloponnese. Minutes before the argument in the hotel room that will threaten to end a relationship cherished by many spectators, Jesse looks at Céline with some perplexity, trying and not managing to fathom the depth of her gaze at the Mediterranean/Ionian Sea. What is going through Céline's mind as she looks pensively, solemnly and contentedly at the sea? Céline's look at the sunset resonates with the comment about the ephemerality of life made at the dinner scene by Natalia (Xenia Kalogeropoulou), one of Patrick's (Walter Lassally) friends, the writer Céline and Jesse are staying with. As Natalia tells them in that scene, she is finding it more and more difficult to conjure up the image of her late husband which, in her mind, appears and disappears 'like a sunrise or a sunset'. Yet, Natalia's tragic view of life, the fact that we are all 'passing through', is counterbalanced by her point that, even in our ephemeral nature, we matter a lot to some: 'we appear and we disappear but we are so important to some'. In this context, the orange light of the sun in front of Céline also evokes the love of life that Patrick had invoked earlier as the central impulse of existence. Delpy's understated performance as she faces the Mediterranean from a Greek coastal town is a contemporary version of the tragic and comic masks of Ancient Greek theatre. She is sitting a few miles away from the stages where the two foundational genres of western theatre were born. Imbued with the spirit of the old actors, Céline, as a fictional construct, may be pondering the meanings of the tragic and the comic in a contemporary context.

In this closing chapter we want to acknowledge the fact that *Before Sunrise* is almost universally considered as part of a trilogy and describe the three films as permeated by a comic perspective. Céline's gaze here links her and Jesse with the young couple that they once were and, simultaneously, reminds us of the resilience of the young lovers within their present selves. Comedy, we will argue, is an apt framework to explain the lasting impact of youth in

DOI: 10.4324/9781003224334-7

people's life and, within the logic of this series, the importance of youth in our culture.

   As other authors have gradually looked at the trilogy as a single entity, the debate around its genericity has often come to the fore. This debate comprises two questions: are the *Before* films trilogy instances of genre cinema or examples of *auteur* cinema? And, if they can indeed be seen as genre cinema, which genre? In his analysis of *Before Sunset*, Leger Grindon acknowledges the conflict between the romantic and the realistic in the film and concludes that its comic vision consists in bringing together the portrayal of realistic doubts about romance and a commitment to its fulfilment (2011: 211, 215). James MacDowell agrees that the films of the trilogy are definitely 'indie' and 'realist' in style but doubts that they can be placed outside conventional generic frameworks. For him, the films engage in a dialogue with Hollywood genres, particularly romantic comedy and melodrama. He argues that the trilogy as a whole can be described as tracing a trajectory from the romcom of *Sunrise* to the melodrama of *Midnight* (2021a: 47–62). Carolina Amaral, for her part, sees the final section of *Midnight* as, rather than rejecting the couple, embracing the complexity and ambiguity of love in duration. This is a view of love that rejects the safe, risk-free type of love that, as she argues following French philosopher Alain Badiou, is the real threat to love in contemporary society (Amaral 2020: 157–8). The films, therefore, remain for her within the frameworks of genre and romantic comedy.

   The debate illustrates the continuing fascination with the formal and narrative mechanisms employed by the films to convey their very powerful impression of reality *and* more general attitudes to genericity, their links with Hollywood cinema and their fit within other cinematic traditions, particularly in this case, *auteur* cinema and European cinema. What is often forgotten in these debates is the long history of some genres outside the cinema, especially romantic comedy and comedy in general. For this reason, it seems particularly apposite that *Midnight* should take place in the cradle of the genre. In occupying this particular space, the filmmakers invite us to soar above specific manifestations of romcom in mainstream cinema and ideologically inflected critical appraisals.

   The origins of comedy have been traced to the *Komos*, a ritualistic procession of revellers of which there is evidence in the seventh century B.C. Authors have connected these events to Dionysus, the god of harvests, vegetation and fertility, as well as insanity and ritual madness. Although there are considerable gaps in the evolution from this rite to Ancient Greek comedy, the construction of comic stories around the force of sexual desire and the celebration of life points in this direction. David Galbraith, following Thomas Lodge, describes comedy in a double guise: a genre whose origins are in ritual celebrations in praise of the gods for a good harvest and one that develops the Ciceronian definition, 'imitation vitae, speculum consuetudinis et imago veritatis' (2002: 4), that would correspond to what theorists of comedy refer to as Aristotelian or satirical comedy, a tradition that has run parallel to and more often than not intersected with romantic comedy. The creation of narratives around the force of sexual desire is the best-known manifestation of a comic vision of the world, but not the only one. This is a vision that includes *eros* but also youth, humour, laughter, resilience, the impulse of survival and the renewal of life. All of these are located, as Andrew Horton and Joanna E. Rapf remind us, in the social and the cultural (2013: 2–4). In other words, it is not just a vital impulse but a way to make sense of our place in society and history, as well as, in the Aristotelian vein, criticise its flaws and contradictions. The qualms that some critics have to acknowledge the strong and, to us, deep links of the trilogy with comedy must be related to recent developments of the genre within popular culture, particularly the cinema but also, for instance, the popular novel and TV, and generalised attitudes towards it that highlight conventionality, repetitiveness, ideological conservativeness and artistic mediocrity (see Deleyto 2009: 24–8). Such authors often forget where romantic comedy comes from and the overriding impulse at the core of the genre: the power of desire, the affirmation of life and the comic impulse, a force that impels us to look at the world through a comic lens, to find humour in the most unexpected circumstances and to laugh at society and ourselves.

'I'm Trying to Make You Laugh'

After she storms out of the hotel room for the third time, we find Céline, pensive and downcast, sitting on a nearby terrace on her own. She is shown in a medium shot and placed to the right of the frame, a framing strategy that emphasises the blank space to her left in what should have been one of the two-shots that we have become accustomed to throughout the trilogy. The stillness of the shot is abruptly broken by the next one: a tracking shot that is soon revealed to be Jesse's movement towards her table. This tracking shot starts with an extreme long shot of Céline and the rest of patrons at the terrace. Among them, a young, long-haired, blonde woman – a dead ringer for the Céline we met in *Before Sunrise* – is leaving the place, frame left, with a bearded young man in a casual T-shirt, just as Jesse enters the frame from the left [see Figures 6.1–6.2]. The characters do not cross paths, but the synchrony between Jesse's and the anonymous characters' movements within the frame resonates with the conversation that follows, one that will impel the protagonists to dive through the layers of frustration and resentment they have accumulated through their nine years together and to remember their encounter in Vienna. If in Vienna they tried to be 'rational adults', in the southern Peloponnese they will have to try to regain contact with their younger selves. The anonymous couple leaving the cafe may evoke their Viennese beginnings and the feelings and emotions that they are now in danger of losing.

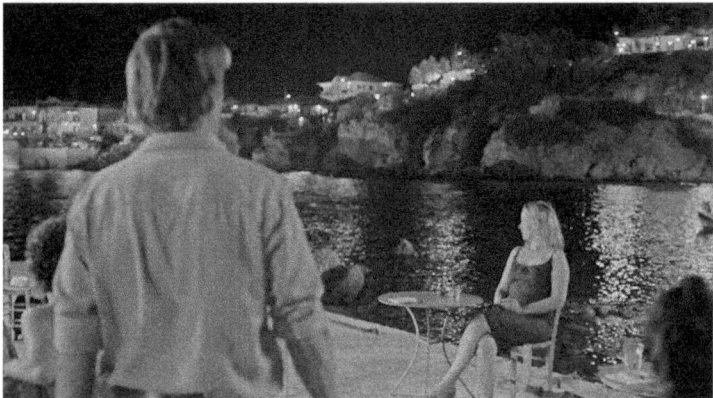

Figures 6.1–6.2 The present and the past of the couple almost cross paths in Greece

As he moves closer to her table, Jesse, playing the role of a stranger, asks
Céline for permission to sit next to her. She grudgingly agrees and impatiently
listens to his made-up story about being a time traveller sent by her 82-year-
old self to save her in that moment of crisis. When Céline tells him that she
does not talk to strangers, he reminds her that he is the same guy she met and
fell in love with in 1994 on a train in Europe, a point that Céline blatantly
dismisses: 'I vaguely remember someone sweet and romantic, who made me
feel like I wasn't alone anymore, someone who had respect for who I was'.
Begrudgingly, Céline listens to the letter her future self has supposedly written to her. The postscript about a night of sex on the southern Peloponnese
is more than Céline can take at this point. She asks Jesse to stop his 'stupid
game'. She angrily reminds him of her last words before leaving the room:

'I don't think I love you anymore', a remark that, as she makes it clear, he should have at least acknowledged. Jesse, however, has chosen to overlook Céline's words and has gone out of the room with reconciliation in mind: 'I'm trying to make you laugh', he claims. Jesse's comic role-playing and his apparent disregard for her words initially infuriate Céline. Yet, as Jesse's attempts at reconciliation begin to run out of steam, she, welling up with tears, finally agrees to play his game and asks him about the time-travel machine he had referred to earlier. While in *Before Sunrise* Jesse's reference to Céline's adult self got her off the train, in *Before Midnight* it is the memories of her younger self that come to the rescue.

Céline's transition from melodrama to comedy in the course of thirty-seven seconds in this scene has been minutely analysed by Deleyto, who emphasises her ability and the actor's power to carry out a transition from anger and resignation to renewed comic zest for life (2023: 148–9) – Jesse must have undergone a similar transition when he goes out of the hotel room but that is kept off-screen. In a two-shot and a long take, the trilogy's favourite stylistic choice since *Before Sunrise*, Jesse and Céline take turns to look at the other and look away, ensuring their eyes never make contact, in an explicit reiteration of the scene at the listening booth in *Before Sunrise* [see Figures 6.3–6.6]. The sexual tension of the first movie has been replaced by sadness, resentment and frustration. Yet, the use of a similar pattern of (non) interaction also shows that, even if the nine years between the second and the third movies of the trilogy have changed them, there are still traces of the two twenty-somethings that once fell in love in Vienna, the choreography of unsynchronised looks paradoxically signalling underlying affinity. Céline had previously noticed in the hotel room that all the red from Jesse's beard (one of the things that she admits made her fall for him in Vienna) is now gone, only to quickly add that now she sees it in their daughters' eyelashes, proving that whatever drove them to each other once may have been reshaped and relocated, but it is still there. Like the philosopher Alain Badiou, the *Before* trilogy presents love as a tenacious adventure, a construction that takes shape and is reshaped over time (2009: 30–2).

   Even if most of the issues that led to their fight in the hotel room are left unresolved by the end of the film, Céline's repeat performance of the admiring 'dumb blonde' makes it clear that both characters, and the film through them, have chosen a comic approach to move on and start anew after their fight. In spite of the emphasis that some critics have placed on the fight to make their readings of *Before Midnight* veer towards the melodramatic, it should be taken into account that neither a fight nor the threat of an imminent separation are alien to comedy. As Wylie Sypher argues in 'The Meanings of Comedy', comedy often 'intersects the orbit of the tragic action without losing its autonomy' (1956: 32). In fact, for Sypher, comedy as a genre is superior to tragic or melodramatic forms because it contains the double action of 'penance and revel' of the fertility rites ('a sacrifice and a feast') that both

Figures 6.3–6.6 Looking back, moving on – the spirit of comedy

Figures 6.3–6.6 (Continued)

comedy and tragedy stem from. What will happen to our fictional couple after this night may be uncertain but, at the end of the film, the magic space of romantic comedy – one that the hotel room, with its impersonal décor, yellowish lighting and beige colour palette, was unable to conjure up – is back in place, casting its protective spell upon the couple.

The link between comedy and a new beginning at the end of *Before Midnight* can be traced back to the Dionysian fertility rites and to some ancient cosmogonies, in which laughter brings about the creation of the world (Santos and Fortea 2018). For Robert W. Corrigan, the ability to start again is intrinsic to the world of comedy, a genre concerned with the fact that 'no matter how many times we may get knocked down or fall short, we somehow manage to pull ourselves up and keep going' (1981: 9). Similarly, Suzanne Langer finds constant regeneration and the impulse to survive at the centre of comedy, which turns the comic rhythm into a celebration of life itself (Langer 1981: 331). For Benjamin Lehman, the comic effect is a felt affirmation about life, which chimes with our intuitive sense of how things are and with our deep human desire to be recreated by seeing 'true humanness prevail, against the frightening altitudes of aspiration, against the set mechanism of the habitual and conventional, against the threat of corruption and of time' (1981: 111).

Regeneration and the Masquerade

In *Before Sunrise* Céline and Jesse were two emerging adults traversing the age of possibilities. Eighteen years later the panoply of possibilities has shrunk considerably as a result of the roads taken and not taken. Jesse's dreams of excellence have not materialised and he seems reasonably content with his job as a writer. In fact, what most troubles him eighteen years on is his inability to forge a meaningful connection with his son, who lives on a different continent.

As he confesses in the letter he pretends to be reading to Céline, he is aware of the fact that he has 'struggled his whole life connecting and being present even with those he loves the most'. Céline, for her part, resents not being able to combine her professional aspirations and motherhood. While young Céline rather naively complained that their generation had nothing to rebel against, the adult one finds more than enough reasons for rebellion in the countless systemic gender inequalities still present in the privileged sector of society she inhabits. By the time of their visit to the southern Peloponnese, both characters have settled for a smaller world and yet, they are still imbued with the spirit of comedy of their younger selves, one that is now revealed to consist in never giving up and adapting to, as the palm-reader in Vienna put it, 'the awkwardness of life'. Adult Jesse resorts to the same time-travel strategy that he used in Vienna to get Céline off the train with him. In Vienna, young Céline was more than ready to play the game and did not take much convincing. Eighteen years later, she is more reluctant but ultimately still willing to make the effort since she knows the game is still worth playing. Like their eighteen-years-younger selves, they still believe that the answer must be in the attempt.

Some critics have claimed that by the end of *Before Midnight*, Jesse and Céline have become the quarrelling couple of the train at the beginning of *Before Sunrise* (Smith 2021b: 22; MacDowell 2021a: 49). Back then, neither Jesse nor Céline had any idea of what the two characters, who spoke German, were arguing about. Eighteen years later, they are experts on the topic. On their first night together in Vienna they referred to most couples' never-ending conversations about the battle of the sexes as a 'skipping record'. Eighteen years later, the same gender quarrelling seems to take up most of their conversations. We never find out what happened to the angry Austrians once they got off the train. But we know that their bickering got Céline and Jesse talking to each other. Their conflict may have been an end (or not) for the Austrian couple, but it brought about a beginning for Céline and Jesse, in a process of displacement that looks like a narrative correlative of the cycle of regeneration that Corrigan, Langer and Lehman see as the defining feature of the comic view of the world.

At this time, eighteen years later, comedy's regenerative powers are at work again. In Céline and Jesse's darkest hour, the film inserts a reminder of their younger selves in the anonymous couple (as anonymous as the Austrian couple) leaving the cafe while Céline is sitting on her own and Jesse enters the frame. This may or may not be a beginning for those two characters, in the same way as it was a beginning for Céline and Jesse eighteen years earlier. It also may or may not be a new beginning for Jesse and Céline, who, in spite of their resentment, their frustrations and the grievances they have hurled at each other in the room, still possess the playful energy and zest for life that brought them together in the first place.

In keeping with the comic spirit that they embody throughout the trilogy, this energy is found in role-playing, their particular version of comedy's well-known trope of the masquerade. From the Q&A games on the tram and at the Viennese cafe, through Céline's performance of Nina Simone at the end of *Before Sunset*, to Jesse's impersonation of the time traveller and Céline's final 'dumb blonde' performance, games and role-playing have been a constant feature of their relationship. As with other disguises, role-playing, and performances in the history of the genre, Jesse and Céline reach, at these moments, for a deeper truth within themselves beyond the realistic scaffolding of the films. Like Shakespearean comic characters, they lose themselves in the masquerade in order to find themselves in a regenerated form. Invariably, their performances, satirical and/or celebratory, invoke the comic within themselves and in the spectators. In this sense, that the trilogy, peppered with various comic acts, should also end with a performance in a Greek setting should give us a reason to ponder on the film's genericity. Indeed, we do not know what is to become of the couple after this balmy summer evening, but that falls outside the film, even if for nine years fans around the world expectantly waited for a new instalment of the series. As it stands, the ending of *Before Midnight* and the trilogy *is* the masquerade and therefore a comic ending, one in which the protagonists, aware of the obstacles, disappointments and betrayals that life has put in their way, still preserve the energy to keep on playing and laughing, and the wisdom to rediscover the magic of youth in and around themselves, not the least in the red hues of their daughters' eyelashes.

In this book, we have argued that the continuing fascination of *Before Sunrise* (and the trilogy) resides in the films' creation of a strong comic space and their affirmation of life within persuasively and painstakingly created realist narratives and in a very specific social and historical context. We have devoted the bulk of the book to the exploration of the film in those contexts, which include the slacker ethos and its European counterpart, late-twentieth century constructions of youthful love and desire and the transnational dimension of the central relationship, all with the process of European construction in a background that gains pace as the trilogy develops. As the three films have succeeded each other in nine-year intervals, the presentness of experience and the passing of time have combined in a very particular, and particularly complex, type of temporality. This contrived temporality coexists with the films' much vaunted 'realist' approach and the very specific cinematic aesthetics on which it is based: extensive work on the script, a carefully orchestrated 'spontaneous' and episodic structure, a very particular type of performance largely indebted to Delpy's and Hawke's cinematic artistry, and the aesthetic choices employed to frame the fictional world. The combination and consistency in the use of these features from *Before Sunrise* onwards underscores the power of the trilogy's comic vision. The walking and talking structure of the films and their curious mixture of a relaxed atmosphere, impending deadlines, and expectations of a cliffhanger at the end are all part of this vision.

The magic space of comedy also permeates the transnational dimension of the story. We have argued that the intimate and the transnational appear closely intertwined in the visual rhetoric of the film. The combination of long takes, shot/reverse shots, close-ups and long shots and, of course, location shooting ensure that, while focusing closely on the two lovers and the little space between them, we never forget the larger world, in this case, represented as much by the real Austrian capital as by the easy cross-border mobility of the characters. Thus considered, the story of the film becomes one about a certain variety of transnational lovers in a city with a long transnational history, one that is unobtrusively evoked by the film's use of particular locations. The year, 1995, in which Austria joined the European Union, was a momentous time for the construction of the new Europe. *Before Sunrise* would in time become part of a trilogy and the characters' encounters in various European places in the course of the two following decades would parallel the ups and downs, hopes and disappointments, of the European project. Following this thread, we have deployed our cosmopolitan analysis of the transnational dimension of the story and of the centrality of the real space of the film to explore the links between the youthful forms of desire between Jesse and Céline and the filmic construction of a young Europe, a territory in which, like the Vienna of the film, tradition informs modernity and coexists with it.

The trilogy's comic lens frames its narrative of youthful love, transnational encounters and European construction. This is a brand of comedy that does not erase or minimise crises, contradictions and frustrated hopes. Rather, it maintains the importance of obstacles and setbacks as part of people's and society's social and emotional experience. In welcoming and convincingly accumulating trouble in the narrative and still remaining firmly in a comic world, the three films become complex cultural texts, boundless in their surface simplicity, and enigmatic in their refusal to settle for univocal interpretations. In *Before Midnight*, Jesse and Céline are in their early forties, have children, commitments and frustrations, but the film continues to convey the same slacker way of relating to the world and coping with obstacles that they embodied, in their transnational differences, eighteen years before. Fans may look sadly at the spectacle of ageing as we follow our heroes from Vienna to Paris and to the Peloponnese but we have no difficulty in rediscovering their younger selves, and consequently our own, as we repeatedly recognise the continuing presence of the two twenty-somethings that met on the train when their world and ours were younger.

Bibliography

Alsop, E. (2021) 'The Radical Middle: *Jane the Virgin, Crazy ExGirlfriend*, and the Subversive Potential of the Television Rom-Com', in M. San Filippo (ed.) *After 'Happily Ever After': Romantic Comedy in the Post-Romantic Age*, Detroit, MI: Wayne State University Press, pp. 219–39.

Amaral, C. (2020) 'Do encontro à duraçao: Amor na trilogia *Antes do amanhecer, Antes do pôr do sol* e *Antes da meia-noite*', *Intexto*, No. 50, pp. 146–60.

Anderson, E. (2011) *The Cosmopolitan Canopy: Race and Civility in Everyday Life*, New York and London: W.W. Norton.

Appiah, K.A. (1997) 'Cosmopolitan Patriots', *Critical Inquiry*, Vol. 23, No. 3, pp. 617–39.

Appiah, K.A. (2018) *The Lies that Bind: Rethinking Identity, Creed, Country, Colour, Class, Culture*, London: Profile Books.

Arnett, J.J. (2004) *Emerging Adulthood: The Winding Road from the Late Teens Through the Twenties*, New York and Oxford: Oxford University Press.

Badiou, A. (2012 [2009]) *In Praise of Love*, London: Serpent's Tail (translated by Peter Bush).

Beck, U. and Sznaider, N. (2006) 'Unpacking Cosmopolitanism for the Social Sciences: A Research Agenda', *The British Journal of Sociology*, Vol. 57, No. 1, pp. 1–23.

Billock, J. (2020) 'Following Beethoven's Footsteps through Vienna', *Smithsonian Magazine*, online, 27 January, https://www.smithsonianmag.com/travel/following -beethovens-footsteps-through-vienna-180973951/.

Borrelli, C. (2013) 'About Time', *Chicago Tribune*, 26 May, pp. 1, 5.

Calhoun, C. (2008) 'Cosmopolitanism and Nationalism', *Nation and Nationalism*, Vol. 14, No. 3, pp. 427–48.

Cenciarelli, C. (2018) 'The Sense of an Ending: Music, Time and Romance in *Before Sunrise*', in L. Bayman and N. Pinazza (eds.) *Journeys on Screen: Theory, Ethics, Aesthetics*, Edinburgh: Edinburgh University Press, pp. 167–82.

Chan, F. (2017) *Cosmopolitan Cinema: Cross-Cultural Encounters in East Asian Film*, London and New York: I.B. Tauris.

Cicchelli, V. (2013) 'The Cosmopolitan "Bildung" of Erasmus Students' Going Abroad', in Y. Hébert and A.A. Abdi (eds.) *Critical Perspectives on International Education*, Rotterdam: SensePublishers Rotterdam, pp. 205–8.

Clark, M.S. and Beck, L.A. (2011) 'Initiating and Evaluating Close Relationships: A Task Central to Emerging Adults', in F.D. Fincham and M. Cui (eds.) *Romantic Relationships in Emerging Adulthood*, Cambridge and New York: Cambridge University Press, pp. 190–212.

Clinton, B. (1994) 'Remarks by President Bill Clinton to the U.C.L.A. 75th Anniversary Convocation [May 20, 1994]', https://www.historycentral.com/documents/DDAY94.html.

Cooper, A. and Rumford, C. (2011) 'Cosmopolitan Borders: Bordering as Connectivity', in M. Rovisco and M. Nowicka (eds.) *The Ashgate Research Companion to Cosmopolitanism*, London: Ashgate, pp. 261–76.

Corrigan, R.W. (1981) 'Introduction: Comedy and the Comic Spirit', in R.W. Corrigan (ed.) *Comedy: Meaning and Form*, New York: Harper and Row, Publishers, pp. 1–11.

Coupland, D. (1991) *Generation X: Tales for an Accelerated Culture*, New York: St. Martin's Press.

Coupland, D. (1995) 'Generation X'd', *Details*, June, p. 72.

Crowther, B. (1957) 'The Screen: *An Affair to Remember*, Stewart Granger Stars in *Gun Glory*', *New York Times*, online, 20 July, https://www.nytimes.com/1957/07/20/archives/the-screen-an-affair-to-remember-stewart-granger-stars-in-gun-glory.html.

Cutler, A. (2013) 'Love in Time: Julie Delpy, Ethan Hawke, and Richard Linklater's *Before* Films', *Cineaste*, Vol. 38, No. 4, pp. 24–8.

Dargis, M. (1995) 'Fools for Love', *LA Weekly*, 2 February, p. 33.

Dargis, M. (2004) 'After Nine Years, did their Hearts Grow Fonder?' *Los Angeles Times*, online, 2 July, https://www.latimes.com/archives/la-xpm-2004-jul-02-et-dargis2-story.html.

Davis, M. (2000) *Magical Urbanism: Latinos Reinvent the U.S. City*, London and New York: Verso.

Delanty, G. (2006) 'The Cosmopolitan Imagination: Critical Cosmopolitanism and Social Theory', *The British Journal of Sociology*, Vol. 57, No. 1, pp. 25–47.

Delanty, G. (2014) 'Not All is Lost in Translation: World Varieties of Cosmopolitanism', *Cultural Sociology*, Vol. 8, No. 4, pp. 1–18.

Deleyto, C. (2009) *The Secret Life of Romantic Comedy*, Manchester: Manchester University Press.

Deleyto, C. (2019) 'Performing Cosmopolitanism: Julie Delpy and Ethan Hawke in Richard Linklater's "Before" Trilogy', *Transnational Screens*, Vol. 10, No. 1, pp. 23–33.

Deleyto, C. (2023) 'Stories so Far: Romantic Comedy and/as Space in *Before Midnight*', in K. Wilkins and T. Vermeulen (eds.) *ReFocus: The Films of Richard Linklater*, Edinburgh: Edinburgh University Press, pp. 136–153.

Figes, O. (2019) *The Europeans: Three Lives and the Making of Cosmopolitan Culture*, London: Penguin.

Fine, R. (2006) 'Cosmopolitanism: A Social Science Research Agenda', in G. Delanty (ed.) *Handbook of Contemporary European Social Theory*, London and New York: Routledge, pp. 242–53.

Fine, R. (2009) 'Cosmopolitanism and Human Rights: Radicalism in a Global Age', *Metaphilosophy*, Vol. 40, No. 1, pp. 8–23.

Fine, R. (2012) 'The Idea of Cosmopolitan Solidarity', in G. Delanty (ed.) *Routledge Handbook of Cosmopolitan Studies*, London and New York: Routledge, pp. 376–86.

Fozdar, F. and Woodward, I. (2021) 'Special Issue Introduction: Post-national Formations and Cosmopolitanism', *Journal of Sociology*, Vol. 57, No. 1, pp. 3–11.

Fussell, P. (1983) *Class: A Guide through the American Status System*, New York and London: Simon and Schuster.

Galbraith, D. (2002) 'Theories of Comedy', in A. Leggatt (ed.) *The Cambridge Companion to Shakespearean Comedy*, Cambridge: Cambridge University Press, pp. 3–17.

Galt, R. (2006) *The New European Cinema: Redrawing the Map*, New York: Columbia University Press.

Gaudin, A. (2015) *L'espace cinématographique: Esthétique et dramaturgie*, Malakoff: Armand Colin.

Giddens, A. (1992) *The Transformation of Intimacy: Sexuality, Love and Eroticism in Modern Societies*, Cambridge and Oxford: Polity Press.

Giroux, H.A. (1996) *Fugitive Cultures: Race, Violence and Youth*, New York and London: Routledge.

Green, S. (2013) 'Introduction', in S. Green and L. Malm (eds.) *Borderwork*, Riga: Silti, pp. 9–17.

Grindon, L. (2011) *The Hollywood Romantic Comedy: Conventions, History, Controversies*, Malden, MA: Wiley-Blackwell.

Gross, D.M. and Scott, S. (1990) 'Living: Proceeding with Caution', *Time*, online, 16 July https://content.time.com/time/subscriber/printout/0,8816,970634,00.html#.

Guccione, B. (1993) 'Unfair Play in the Generation Wars: Twentysomethings Don't Deserve the Negativity Rap from their Elders, the Sell-out '60s Crowd and the Selfish Boomers', *Los Angeles Times*, online, 21 February, https://www.latimes.com/archives/la-xpm-1993-02-21-op-729-story.html.

Hamblett, C. and Deverson, J. (1964) *Generation X*, Greenwich, CT: Gold Medal Books.

Hanson, P. (2002) *The Cinema of Generation X: A Critical Study of Films and Directors*, Jefferson, NC and London: McFarland and Company.

Harrod, M., Liz, M. and Timoshkina, A., (2015) 'The Europeanness of European Cinema: An Overview', in M. Harrod, M. Liz and A. Timoshkina (eds.) *The Europeanness of European Cinema: Identity, Meaning, globalisation*, London and New York: I.B. Tauris, pp. 1–15.

Haworth, J.G. (1997) 'The Misrepresentation of Generation X', *About Campus: Enriching the Student Learning Experience*. Vol. 2, No. 4, pp. 10–15.

Haynes, L. (1957) '"Affair to Remember": Brittle Dialog Pleases', *Independent – Star News*, 4 August, p. 15.

Heiman, R.J. (2001) 'The Ironic Contradictions in the Discourse on Generation X: Or How "Slackers" are Saving Capitalism', *Childhood*, Vol. 8, No. 2, pp. 274–92.

Horton, A. and Rapf, J.E. (2013) 'Comic Introduction: 'Make 'em Laugh, Make 'em Laugh!', in A. Horton and J.E. Rapf (eds.) *A Companion to Film Comedy*, Malden, MA: Wiley-Blackwell, pp. 1–11.

Høy-Petersen, N. and Woodward, I. (2018) 'Working with Difference: Cognitive Schemas, Ethical Cosmopolitanism and Negotiating Cultural Diversity', *International Sociology*, Vol. 33, No. 6, pp. 655–73.

Isola, M.J. (2013) 'From Dropout to Doctor: A Slacker Slacking in Academia', in E. Watson (ed.) *Generation X Professors Speak: Voices from Academia*, Lanham, MD and Toronto: Scarecrow Press, pp. 133–50.

Jeffers McDonald, T. (2007) *Romantic Comedy: Boy Meets Girl Meets Genre*, London and New York: Wallflower.

Kehr, D. (1993) 'In Slacker Films, Passing Time Is the Primary Pastime', *Chicago Tribune*, online, 16 May, https://www.chicagotribune.com/news/ct-xpm-1993-05 -16-9305160454-story.html.

Keogh, P. (2000 [1992]) 'Death and Hollywood', in D. Sterritt (ed.) *Robert Altman Interviews*, Jackson, MS: University Press of Mississippi, pp. 156–62.

King, G. (2005) *American Independent Cinema*, London: I.B. Tauris.

Kluft, D. (2014) 'When "Slacker" Was a Dirty Word: Defamation and Draft Dodging during World War I', *Foley Hoag's Trademark & Copyright Law*, online, 30 June, https://www.trademarkandcopyrightlawblog.com/2014/06/when-slacker-was-a -dirty-word-defamation-and-draft-dodging-during-world-war-i/.

Konstantarakos, M. (2000) 'Introduction', in M. Konstantarakos (ed.) *Spaces in European Cinema*, London: Intellect, pp. 3–6.

Kopkind, A. (1992) 'Slacking Toward Bethlehem', *Grand Street*, No. 44, pp. 176–88.

Krutnik, F. (1990) 'The Faint Aroma of Performing Seals: The "Nervous" Romance and the Comedy of the Sexes', *Velvet Light Trap*, No. 26, pp. 57–72.

Langer, S. (1981 [1953]) 'The Comic Rhythm', in R.W. Corrigan (ed.) *Comedy: Meaning and Form*, New York: Harper and Row, Publishers, pp. 67–83.

Lee, C. (2010) *Screening Generation X: The Politics and Popular Memory of Youth in Contemporary Cinema*, Surrey and Burlington: Ashgate.

Lefebvre, H. (1991 [1974]) *The Production of Space*, Oxford and Malden, MA: Blackwell (translated by Donald Nicholson-Smith).

Lehmann, B. (1981 [1954]) 'Comedy and Laughter', in R.W. Corrigan (ed.) *Comedy: Meaning and Form*, New York: Harper and Row, Publishers, pp. 100–111.

Lejeune, C.A. (1939) 'Films of the Week', *Observer*, 16 April, p. 12.

Lent, T.O. (1995) 'Romantic Love and Friendship: The Redefinition of Gender Relations in Screwball Comedy', in *Classical Hollywood Comedy*. New York: Routledge, pp. 314–32.

Levy, E. (1999) *Cinema of Outsiders: The Rise of American Independent Film*, New York and London: New York University Press.

Linklater, R. (2020 [1991]) 'From the Archives: Linklater on Linklater', *Austin Chronicle*, online, 24 July, https://www.austinchronicle.com/screens/2020-07-24/ from-the-archives-linklater-on-linklater/.

MacDowell, J. (2008) 'Love and Fate in *The Clock* and *Before Sunrise*', *Alternate Takes*, online, http://www.alternatetakes.co.uk/?2008,1,194.

MacDowell, J. (2013) *Happy Endings in Hollywood Cinema: Cliché, Convention and the Final Couple*, Edinburgh: Edinburgh University Press.

MacDowell, J. (2017) 'To Be in the Moment: On (Almost) Not Noticing Time Passing in *Before Sunrise* (Richard Linklater 1995)', in J. Gibbs and D. Pye (eds.) *The Long Take*, London: Palgrave Macmillan, pp. 147–61.

MacDowell, J. (2021a) 'Comedy and Melodrama from *Sunrise* to *Midnight*: Gender and Genre in Linklater's *Before* Series', in M. San Filippo (ed.) *After 'Happily Ever After': Romantic Comedy in the Postromantic Age*, Detroit, MI: Wayne State University Press, pp. 47–66.

MacDowell, J. (2021b) 'Romance, Narrative and the Sense of a Happy Ending in the *Before* Series', in H. Maes and K. Schaubroeck (eds.) *Before Sunrise, Before Sunset, Before Midnight: A Philosophical Exploration*, London and New York: Routledge, pp. 174–93.

Macor, A. (2010) *Chainsaws, Slackers, and Spy Kids: 30 Years of Filmmaking in Austin, Texas*, Austin, TX: University of Texas Press.

Maes, H. (2021) 'A Trilogy of Melancholy: On the Bittersweet in *Before Sunrise, Before Sunset* and *Before Midnight*', in H. Maes and K. Schaubroeck (eds.) *Before Sunrise, Before Sunset, Before Midnight: A Philosophical Exploration*, London and New York: Routledge, pp. 41–64.

Magris, C. (2017 [1986]) *Danube*, London: The Harvill Press.

Massey, D. (2005) *For Space*, Los Angeles, CA and London: Sage.

McCann, B. (2018) *L'auberge espagnole: European Youth on Film*, London: Routledge.

Mignolo, W.D. (2011) 'Border Thinking, Decolonial Cosmopolitanism and Dialogues among Civilizations', in M. Rovisco and M. Nowicka (eds.) *The Ashgate Research Companion to Cosmopolitanism*, London: Ashgate, pp. 329–47.

Naficy, H. (2001) *An Accented Cinema: Exilic and Diasporic Filmmaking*, Princeton, NJ: Princeton University Press.

Naficy, H. (2006) 'Situating Accented Cinema', in E. Ezra and T. Rowden (eds.) *Transnational Cinema: The Film Reader*, London and New York: Routledge, pp. 111–30.

Neale, S. (1992) 'The Big Romance or Something Wild? Romantic Comedy Today', *Screen*, Vol. 33, No. 3, pp. 284–99.

Neupert, R. (1995) *The End: Narration and Closure in the Cinema*, Detroit, MI: Wayne State University Press.

Norton, G. (2000) 'The Seductive Slack of *Before Sunrise*', *Post Script*, Vol. 19, No. 2, pp. 62–72.

Norwich, J.J. (2006) *The Middle Sea*, London: Chatto & Windus.

Nowell-Smith, G. (2001) 'Cities: Real and Imagined', in M. Shiel and T. Fitzmaurice (eds.) *Cinema and the City: Film and Urban Societies in a Global Context*, Oxford: Blackwell, pp. 99–108.

Nyers, P. (2003) 'Abject Cosmopolitanism: The Politics of Protection in the Anti-Deportation Movement', *Third World Quarterly*, Vol. 24, No. 6, pp. 1069–93.

Oria, B. (2018) 'Love on the Margins: The American Indie Rom-com of the 2010s', *Atlantis*, Vol. 40, No. 2, pp. 145–67.

Oria, B. (2021) 'We Found Love in a Hopeless Place: Romantic Comedy of the Post-Romantic Era', in M. San Filippo (ed.) *After 'Happily Ever After': Romantic Comedy in the Post-Romantic Age*, Detroit, MI: Wayne State University Press, pp. 27–46.

Ortner, S.B. (1998) 'Generation X: Anthropology in a Media Saturated World', *Cultural Anthropology*, Vol. 13, No. 3, pp. 414–40.

Pierson, J. (2014 [1995]) *Spike, Mike, Slackers and Dykes: A Guided Tour across a Decade of American Independent Cinema*, Austin: University of Texas Press.

Rhodes, J.D. and Gorfinkel, E. (2011) 'Introduction: The Matter of Places', in J.D. Rhodes and E. Gorfinkel (eds.) *Taking Place: Location and the Moving Image*, Minneapolis, MN and London: University of Minnesota Press, pp. vii–xxix.

Ritchie, K. (1995) *Marketing to Generation X*, New York and London: Lexington Books.

Robbins, B. (1998) 'Introduction to Part I: Actually Existing Cosmopolitanism', in P. Cheah and B. Robbins (eds.) *Cosmopolitics: Thinking and Feeling Beyond the Nation*, Minneapolis, MN: University of Minnesota Press, pp. 1–19.

Roberts, S. (2019) 'Reality Bites Captured Generation X with Perfect Irony', *The Atlantic*, online, 20 March, https://www.theatlantic.com/entertainment/archive/2019/03/reality-bites-captured-gen-x-25-years-later-helen-childress/583870/.

Robertson, A. (2012) 'Media Cultures and Cosmopolitan Connections', in G. Delanty (ed.) *The Routledge Handbook of Cosmopolitan Studies*, London and New York: Routledge, pp. 178–87.

Rovisco, M. (2013) 'Towards a Cosmopolitan Cinema: Understanding the Connection Between Borders, Mobility and Cosmopolitanism in the Fiction Film', *Mobilities*, Vol. 8, No. 1, pp. 148–65.

Ruiz-Domènec, J.E. (2022) *El sueño de Ulises: El Mediterráneo, de la guerra de Troya a las Pateras*, Madrid: Taurus.

Rushkoff, D. (1994) 'Introduction: Us, by Us', in D. Rushkoff (ed.) *The GenX Reader*, New York: Ballantine Books, pp. 3–8.

Safire, W. (1994) 'On Language: Cut Them Some Slack', *New York Times*, online, 3 July, https://www.nytimes.com/1994/07/03/magazine/on-language-cut-them-some-slack.html.

San Filippo, M. (2015) 'Growing Old Together: Linklater's *Before* Trilogy in the Twilight Years of Art House Distribution', *Film Quarterly*, Vol. 68, No. 3, pp. 53–9.

San Filippo, M. (2021) 'Love Actually: Romantic Comedy Since the Aughts', in M. San Filippo (ed.) *After 'Happily Ever After': Romantic Comedy in the Post-Romantic Age*, Detroit, MI: Wayne State University Press, pp. 1–24.

Santos Saavedra, J. and Fortea Bastart, R. (2018) 'And Everything Began with Laughs and Tears… The Creation of the Gods According to Esna II, 163, 16–17; III 206, 8–9 and III, 272, 2–3: Precedents, Interpretations and Influences', *Trabajos de Egiptología*, No. 9, pp. 187–206.

Savlov, M. (2011) 'Slack to the Future: Austin Gets Older; "Slacker" Stays Forever Young', *The Austin Chronicle*, online, 21 January, https://www.austinchronicle.com/screens/2011-01-21/slack-to-the-future/.

Schallert, E. (1939) 'Love Affair Acclaimed in Preview', *Los Angeles Times*, 10 March, p. 14.

Shaw, D. (2013) 'Deconstructing and Reconstructing "Transnational Cinema"', in S. Dennison (ed.) *Contemporary Hispanic Cinema: Interrogating the Transnational in Spanish and Latin American Film*, Woodbridge: Tamesis, pp. 47–65.

Skrbiš, Z. and Woodward, I. (2013) *Cosmopolitanism: Uses of the Idea*, Los Angeles, CA, London, New Delhi, Singapore, and Washington, DC: Sage.

Smith, M. (2021b) 'The Poetry of Day-to-Day Life', in H. Maes and K. Schaubroeck (eds.) *Before Sunrise, Before Sunset, Before Midnight: A Philosophical Exploration*, London and New York: Routledge, pp. 6–23.

Smith, M. (2021a) 'Epic Intimacy', in H. Maes and K. Schaubroeck (eds.) *Before Sunrise, Before Sunset, Before Midnight: A Philosophical Exploration*, London and New York: Routledge, pp. 83–101.

Spencer, A. (2020) 'Before Sunrise: The Making of an Indie Classic', *New York Times*, online, 22 January, https://www.nytimes.com/2020/01/22/movies/before-sunrise-ethan-hawke-julie-delpy.html.

Stacey, J. (2017) 'The Uneasy Cosmopolitans of *Code Unknown*', in N. Glick Schiller and A. Irving (eds.) *Whose Cosmopolitanism? Critical Perspectives, Relationalities and Discontents*, New York and Oxford: Berghahn, pp. 160–74.

Sternberg, J. (2002) 'I Didn't Get It, But I Liked the Name: Generational Profiling through Generation X', in M. Balnaves, T. O'Regan and J. Sternberg (eds.) *Mobilising the Audience*, Brisbane: University of Queensland Press, pp. 81–103.

Stone, R. (2007) 'Between Sunrise and Sunset: An Elliptical Dialogue Between American and European Cinema', in P. Cooke (ed.) *World Cinema's 'Dialogues' with Hollywood*, Hampshire and New York: Palgrave-MacMillan, pp. 218–37.

Stone, R. (2013) *The Cinema of Richard Linklater: Walk, Don't Run*, London and New York: Wallflower Press.

Stone, R. (2018) *The Cinema of Richard Linklater: Walk, Don't Run*, 2nd edition, New York: Columbia University Press.

Strauss, W. and Howe, N. (1991) *Generations: The History of America's Future, 1584 to 2069*, New York and London: Harper.

'Sunrise over Criticism' (1995) *Austin American-Stateman*, 9 February, pp. 52, 58.

Swidler, A. (2001) *Talk of Love: How Culture Matters*, Chicago, IL and London: University of Chicago Press.

Sypher, W. (1956) *Comedy*, Baltimore, MD and London: The Johns Hopkins University Press.

Tretter, E. (2020) 'The Slacker Colonialist and the Gentrification of Austin', *The End of Austin*, online, 21 November, https://endofaustin.com/2020/11/21/the-slacker-colonialist-and-the-gentrification-of-austin/.

Tzioumakis, Y. (2017 [2006]) *American Independent Cinema*, 2nd edition, Edinburgh: Edinburgh University Press.

Ulrich, J.M. (2003) 'Introduction: Generation X, A (Sub)cultural Genealogy', in J.M. Ulrich and A.L. Harris (eds.) *GenXegesis: Essays on Alternative Youth (Sub) Culture*, Madison, WI: University of Wisconsin Press/Popular Press, pp. 3–37.

Viera, M.A. (2013) *Majestic Hollywood: The Greatest Films of 1939*, Philadelphia, PA: Running Press.

Wales, C. (1939) 'Love Affair', *Screen and Radio Weekly*, Section of Detroit Free Press, 12 March, p. 5.

Whelan, R. (1985) *Robert Capa: A Biography*, Lincoln, NE: University of Nebraska Press.

White, B. (1946) 'McCarey Rated Tops for Trophy', *Los Angeles Times*, 13 January, p. 23.

Wilmington, M. (1995) 'Sleepless in Vienna', *Chicago Tribune*, 27 January, p. C.

Winiwarter, V., Schmid, M. and Dressel, G. (2013) 'Looking at Half a Millennium of Co-existence: The Danube in Vienna as a Socio-Natural Site', *Water History*, Vol. 5, No. 2, pp. 101–19.

Wood, R. (1998) *Sexual Politics and Narrative Film: Hollywood and Beyond*, New York: Columbia University Press.

Index

Already Tomorrow in Hong Kong
(Ting, 2015) 20, 40
Amaral, Carolina 72
An Affair to Remember (McCarey,
1957) 18, 26, 28, 33–34, 37
An American in Paris (Minnelli,
1951) 58
Andante (Bach) 29–30, 32
Anderson, Elijah 48
Annie Hall (Allen) 17
Antonioni, Michelangelo 53
Arnett, Jeffrey 9, 35
Austin (Texas) 11, 39
Austria 55, 70; *see also* Vienna

Baby Boomers 7
Badiou, Alain 75
Beautiful Girls (Demme, 1996)
12, 39
Beck, Lindsey A. 35
Beck, Ulrich 41
Before Midnight (Linklater, 2013) 1,
16, 19, 22, 24, 46, 53, 55, 70–73,
74, 75, *76–77*
Before Sunrise (Linklater, 1995) 1,
9, 15–16, 18, 21, 23, 58; attitudes
towards love/relationships in
36–37; bar scene 33, *34*, 35–37,
38; borders in 44, 46; casting 21;
compared to *Before Midnight*
74–75, 77–78; and
cosmopolitanism 44–45, 52;
elderly characters in 31, *32*; ending
28–30, 32, 56; 'Europeanness' of
58; importance of dialogue in 5;
inspiration for 13, 16; and *Love
Affair* 27–28, 33–34, 37 39–40;
park night scene 45, *46*; realism in

18, 28–29, 37, 64; referencing other
movies 27; as romantic comedy
18–20, 22, 29, 46, 48, 72; script
20–22, 25–26, 39–40; setting 21;
and *Slacker* 23; and slackers 12–13,
47–48; soundtrack 29–30, 32–33,
37, 56, 60–61, 63; stylistic choices
4, 45–46, 48–49, *50–51*, 53, 80;
temps mort sequence 30–31; and
trains 59–61; and *Ulysses* 11
Before Sunset (Linklater, 2004) 1,
11, 22–23, 27, 32–33, 35, 46, 55,
58, 70, 79
Before trilogy 1–2, 4, 9, 15–16,
18–19, 22–24, 26, 31, 40, 44,
54–55, 59, 70–72, 79–80
Bergson, Henri 18–19
borders 40, 43–44, 46, 54
border thinking 42–44
borderwork 44, 59
Boyer, Charles 25, 28
Boyhood (Linklater, 2014) 10
The Brothers McMullen (Burns,
1995) 12, 20, 39
Burns, Edward 14, 19–20

Calhoun, Craig 42
Capa, Robert 6–7
Castle Rock 15, 18, 21
Céline (character) 1, 9, 12, 29–30,
32, 46, *50–51*, 58, 62, 70;
background of 5, 28, 47, 57;
in *Before Midnight* 59, 73,
74, 75, *76*, 78, 80; casting 21;
conversations 40, 45–46, 48–49,
78; emotional expressions of 4,
37, *38*, 49; meeting Jesse 4–5,
35–36, 57–58, 60; relationship

with Jesse 18, 26–27, 30, 34, 63, 67, 71; as slacker 12–13
Cenciarelli, Carlo 30, 32, 60
Chan, Felicia 43
Chasing Amy (Smith, 1997) 12
Cicchelli, Vincenzo 57
city films 53
Class: A Guide through the American Status System (Fussell) 7
Clerks (Smith, 1994) 12
The Clock (Minnelli, 1945) 64
Columbia Pictures 15
comedy 71–73, 75, 77–78, 80; in *Before Midnight* 74–75, 79; in *Before Sunrise* 78–79
'confessional comedies' 19
Cooper, Anthony 43–44
Corrigan, Robert W. 77–78
cosmopolitan canopy 48
cosmopolitanism 41–46, 52, 58–59, 80
cosmopolitan theory 41, 43
Coupland, Douglas 7–9
Crowe, Cameron 12
Crowther, Bosley 26
Cutler, Aaron 28–29

Danube river 32, 51–52, 56, 60–62, 67, *68*, 69
Dargis, Manohla 35
Davis, Mike 44
Dazed and Confused (1993) 15–16, 20–21, 39
Debord, Guy 11, 18, 47
Delanty, Gerard 41–42, 46
Deleuze, Gilles 18
Deleyto, Celestino 19, 75
Delpy, Julie 1, 21, 25–26, 28, 35, 39, 49, 75, 79; *see also* Céline (character)
dérive 47–48, 58
Detour Productions 15
dialogue: Linklater's use of 5, 22; between US and European cinema 24
Dido and Aeneas (Purcell) 29, 60–61
Dunne, Irene 25, 28
durée 47–48

'emerging adulthood' 9, 35, 38
endings 29–30
Enough Said (Holofcener, 2013) 19
Erasmus program 24, 57, 62
Eurocentrism 42
Europe 54–59, 69, 80; *see also* Danube river
European cinema 19, 24, 54, 58
European Union 21, 54–55

Figes, Orlando 59, 61, 69
Fine, Robert 41, 47
500 Days of Summer (Webb, 2009) 20, 40
Friends (1994-2004) 12
Friends with Money (Holofcener, 2006) 19

Galt, Rosalind 54–55
Gaudin, Antoine 52, 54
'Gen-X genre' 5–6
Generation X: concerns of 7, 9; demographics 7–8; slacker culture 11–12, 16, 18, 38, 47–48, 58; stereotypes 8–9, 11, 35; term history 6, 8–9; *see also* youth cultures
Generation X : Tales for an Accelerated Culture (Coupland) 7–8
Generation X (Hamblett and Deverson) 6
The Generation X Reader (Rushkoff) 9
genre conventions 19–20
genres 19, 72–73
GenXegesis (Ulrich) 6
Giddens, Anthony 30, 36–37
globalisation 42, 59
Grant, Cary 26, 28
Green, Sarah 44
Grindon, Leger 72
The Groomsmen (Burns, 2006) 20

Hamblett, Charles 6–7
Happy Accidents (Anderson, 2000) 26
Harrod, Mary 24

Hawke, Ethan 1, 5–6, 10, 21, 35, 39, 79; *see also* Jesse (character)
Hawks, Howard 15
heterosexual desire, stories of 20
Holiday 6
Hollywood 15, 17–19, 72
Holofcener, Nicole 12, 19
Horton, Andrew 73
Høy-Petersen, Nina 43

independent cinema 15, 23, 45, 58; defining 14; and Hollywood 15, 17–18, 72; and love/desire 16–17; and parodies 17; and romantic comedies 17, 19–20; settings 39
In Search of a Midnight Kiss (Holdridge, 2007) 20, 40
Irreconcilable Differences (Shyer, 1984) 26
It's Impossible to Learn to Plow by Reading Books (Linklater, 1988) 10, 15–16

Jeffers McDonald, Tamar 17
Jesse (character) 1, 9, 12, 32, 38, 59, 62, 70; appearance 6, *50–51* ; background of 5, 28, 47, 57–58; in the bar scene 33–34; in *Before Midnight* 59, 73, *74*, 75, *76*, 77–78, 80; casting 21; conversations 40, 45–46, 48–49, 64, 78; meeting Céline 4–5, 35–36, 57–58, 60; relationship with Céline 18, 26–27, 30, 34, 63, 67, 71; as slacker 12–13, 58
Journey to Italy (Rossellini, 1954) 53, 55

Kerr, Deborah 26, 28
Kicking and Screaming (Baumbach, 1995) 12–13
King, Geoff 17
Krizan, Kim 20–22
Krutnik, Frank 17

Langer, Suzanne 77–78
La Notte (Antonioni, 1961) 53, 55
Lassally, Walter 71

L'auberge espagnol (Klapisch, 2002) 57
L'Eclisse (Antonioni, 1962) 56
Lefebvre, Henri 55
Lehman, Benjamin 77–78
Letter from an Unknown Woman (Ophüls, 1948) 60–61, 66
Levy, Emmanuel 14
Linklater, Richard 1, 6, 8–10, 14, 39; *Before Sunrise* inspiration 16; *Before Sunrise* script 20–21; as indie film maker 14–15; on romantic comedies 17–18; and 'slacker' 9–10, 13, 33, 47; use of dialogue 5, 22; *see also specific films*
'little space in between' 46, 48–49
location shooting 53–55, 61–62, 67, 70, 80
Lodge, Thomas 72–73
long takes 45
Love Affair (McCarey, 1939) 18, 25–28, 33–34, 37
love/desire 16–17
love/relationships 35–38, 72
Lovely & Amazing (Holofcener, 2001) 19
Lovers of the Arctic Circle (Medem, 1998) 55

McCarey, Leo 25–27
MacDowell, James 27, 29–30, 35–36, 45, 59, 64, 72
Magris, Claudio 62, 66, 68–69
Making Love (Hiller, 1982) 26
Mamma Mia! (Lloyd, 2008) 58
Manhattan (Allen) 17
Marketing to Generation X (Ritchie) 7–8
Massey, Doreen 54
Mignolo, Walter 42–44, 47
Minnelli, Vincente 15
mise-en-scène 53–54, 61, *68*
'Mitteleuropa' 69–70
Monsters (Edwards, 2010) 20, 40
Mrs. Slacker (Henley, 1918) 10

Naficy, Hamid 44
Neale, Steve 26

neoliberal capitalism 11
Neupert, Richard 29–30
Norton, Glen 5–6, 28
Notting Hill (Michell, 1999) 17
nouvelle vague 10–11, 18–19, 58
Nowell-Smith, Geoffrey 53–56
Nyers, Peter 43

One, Two, Three (Wilder, 1961) 58
Open Story films 29–30
Oria, Beatriz 20
Orion Classics 15

Paris 55, 70
parodies 17
'Philadelphia story' 16, 21–22
pink champagne 27, 33–34
Pretty Woman (Marshall, 1990) 17
Purcell, Henry 29, 60–61

rail travel 56–57, 59–61
Rapf, Joanna E. 73
realism 18–19, 23, 28–29; in *Before
Sunrise* 18, 28–29, 64; in *Love
Affair* (1939) 25, 37
Reality Bites (Stiller) 5–6, 10, 12
Romancing the Stone (Zemeckis,
1985) 17
Roman Holiday (Wyler, 1953) 58
romantic comedies 4, 16–17, 19–20;
and *Before Midnight* 77; and
Before Sunrise 18–20, 22, 29, 46,
48, 72; Linklater on 17–18; 'new
romances' 26–27
romantic relationships 36–37
*Romy and Michele's High School
Reunion* (Mirkin, 1997) 39
Rossellini, Roberto 53
Rovisco, Maria 44
Ruby in Paradise (Nunez, 1993) 39
Rumford, Christopher 43–44
Ryder, Wynona 10

San Antonio (Texas) 13, 21, 39
San Filippo Maria 14–15, 19–20, 23
sex, lies, and videotape (Soderbergh,
1989) 16
Shafer, Martin 15, 18
She's the One (Burns, 1996) 12–13

Sidewalks of New York (Burns,
2001) 20
Singles (Crowe) 12, 39
Skrbiš, Zlatko 42
slacker 9–12, 16, 47
Slacker (1991) 5–8, 12–16, 23,
33–34, 39, 47
The Slacker (Cabanne, 1917) 10
slacker culture 11–12, 16, 18, 38,
47–48, 58
The Slacker's Heart (Ireland,
1917) 10
Sleepless in Seattle (Ephron, 1993)
17, 26
Smith, Murray 27
Something Wild (Demme, 1986) 17
*Sonata for Viola da Gamba and
Harpsichord* BWV 1027 (Bach) 29
space 54–55
Splash! (Howard, 1984) 17
Stacey, Jackie 41–42, 47
Stone, Rob 10–11, 13–14, 18–19,
24, 27, 47, 58
Sundance 15, 23
Sypher, Wylie 75, 77
Sznaider, Nathan 41

Talk of Love (Swidler, 2001) 35–36
Tarantino, Quentin 14
temporality 19, 23
temps mort 30–31, 47–48, 51, 58
The Bourne Identity (Liman, 2002) 58
The Third Man (Reed, 1949) 66
Ting, Emily 40
Touch of Pink (Rashid, 2004) 26
trains 56–57, 61; and *Before Sunrise*
59–60
transnational culture 39, 41, 43
transnational films 2, 9, 23–24, 40,
43–44, 59, 79–80
transnationality 23–24, 40–41, 43,
55, 80
Transnational Screens 40
Trouble in Paradise (Lubitsch,
1932) 27
The Truth about Cats and Dogs
(Lehman, 1996) 39
Tzioumakis, Yannis 14

Ulrich, John M. 6–7

Vartan, Michael 21
Vicky Cristina Barcelona (Allen, 2008) 58
Vienna 23, *31*, 39, 51, 62–64, 70; in *Before Sunrise* 30, *32–33*, 34, 44–45, 48–49, *50–51,* 51–52, 55–56, 62, *63–65,* 66–67
Vienna film festival 21

Waking Life (Linklater) 6
Walking and Talking (Holofcener, 1996) 12, 19, 39

When Harry Met Sally (Reiner, 1989) 17
While You Were Sleeping (Turteltaub, 1995) 17
'Wiener Blut' waltz (Strauss) 37
Wilmington, Michael 34
Wood, Robin 18, 27–28, 30, 45
Woodward, Ian 42–43
Working Girl (Nichols, 1988) 17

You've Got Mail (Ephron, 1998) 17

For Product Safety Concerns and Information please contact our EU
representative GPSR@taylorandfrancis.com
Taylor & Francis Verlag GmbH, Kaufingerstraße 24, 80331 München, Germany

www.ingramcontent.com/pod-product-compliance
Lightning Source LLC
Chambersburg PA
CBHW071056280326
41928CB00050B/2530

9 781032 123936